LAODICEAN WHOREDOM IN TODAY'S CHURCH

Sonia R. Anderson

Copyright © 2014 by Sonia R. Anderson

Unless otherwise indicated, Scripture quotations taken from the 21st Century King James Version®, copyright © 1994. Used by permission of Deuel Enterprises, Inc., Gary, SD 57237. All rights reserved.

"Scripture quotations taken from the New American Standard Bible®,
Copyright © 1960, 1962, 1963, 1968, 1971, 1972, 1973, 1975, 1977, 1995 by The Lockman Foundation
Used by permission." (www.Lockman.org)

Cover Design by Joshua Cullins

No portion of this book or its cover may be reproduced or transmitted in any form except by written permission and consent of the author.

Laodicean Whoredom in Today's Church
By Sonia R. Anderson

ISBN: 978-0-9936879-0-7
ISBN: 978-0-9936879-1-4 (e-book)

Published by Elect Lady Publishing House
Toronto, Ontario Canada

LAODICEAN WHOREDOM IN TODAY'S CHURCH

AN URGENT CALL TO REPENTANCE

Come now, and let us reason together, saith the LORD: though your sins be as scarlet, they shall be as white as snow: though they be red like crimson, they shall be as wool.
Isaiah 1:18

Dedication

First off, to my Lord and Saviour Jesus Christ. In Him I live and move and have my being.

To the body of Christ: I am honoured to be a part of the Family of God.

To the pastors and leaders who have disciple me in the things and ways of God…Thank you.

To my grandmother and parents: My first instructors who groomed my life for God.

Special thanks to Angella and Carcia for editing my work.

I give the Lord Jesus Christ thanks for my children: Jamae, Pierre, Andre, my son-in-law Joshua and grandchildren Shua and Gianna. You have enriched my life. I encourage you to walk before God and be holy.

Contents

Prayer 8

Introduction 10

1: Darkness in the Church 19

2: Offering of Dead Foul Sacrifices to God 25

3: Spirit of Slumber 30

4: Spirit of Envy 35

5: Off Course, Out of Range 41

6: Satanic Symbol 47

7: Laodicea Whores in Today's Church 55

8: Empty Baptismal Pool 59

9: Field of Rotten Veggies 99

10: Bodies in the Sky 108

11: Demons among the Children 115

12: Sorcery in the Church 129

13: Praying Demonic Prayers 138

14: Sold to the Highest Bidders 147

15: The Face in the Sky Preaching the Gospel 153

16: Welcome to Today's Laodicea Church 161

17: Conclusion of the Matter	176
18: Repentance Call	184
19: Prayer of Repentance	188
About the Author	191

Prayer

Our Heavenly Father, in the mighty name of our Lord Jesus Christ, we glorify and bless You. Thank you for sending Your Son, the Lord Jesus Christ to be crucified for the world. Father, You loved the world so much that You sent Him to die so that we may have everlasting life, as it is recorded in St. John 3:16. Father, as every person reads through the pages of this book, open their eyes to see, open their ears to hear and their understanding, so that they may comprehend what You desire of the Church. Grant each person a heart of repentance, for your goodness leads us to repentance as stated in Romans 2:4.

Father, in Romans 8:26 the Spirit helps our infirmities and makes intercessions for us even in regards to these conditions. Jesus Christ has already nailed all of our sins to the cross as mentioned in Colossians 2:14. Lord Jesus, I bring all people of every nation, in every religious persuasion and non-religious persuasion to You, that all may come to know You, the one true God.

Our Father, let these words written in this book take wings and fly to every corner of the earth. Let the wind of God blow them quickly that it may reach all ears, so that we may quickly turn to God and be saved.

Thank you Heavenly Father, in the Almighty name of our Lord Jesus Christ. Amen.

Introduction

Dream

I was somewhere outside when I looked up in the sky and saw a circle carved out in the sky. The face of Jesus Christ appeared in the circle. The light that was radiating from Him was so bright that it blocked the view of His face to such a degree that I was unable to look directly in His face. There was light glaring in and around the circle and Jesus Christ began to speak to me. At this time I was no longer standing on the earth but was suspended in space and felt a force that was more powerful than I, drawing me closer to the circle. The closer I got to the circle the brighter the light became. He said a lot of things to me, voicing His concerns about what was happening in the church and the earth. I said to Him, "What do you want me to do?" He said, "The harvest is full, I need you to reap." I said, "What must I use?" Immediately and unexpectedly a hand came out of the circle with a Bible and extended it to me. The Bible was open with its leaves flapping as if the wind was blowing on it but there wasn't any wind blowing. It was alive and had a life of its own, moving on its own accord. The light radiating from the Bible was so bright. There were flames of fire ascending from its pages, although it did not burn them. The

Introduction

Bible was placed in my hands from the hand that was extended out of the circle of light. I took it out of His hand. Although it was shooting flames of fire it did not burn me. It was alive! I woke up immediately upon receiving the Bible.

For several months in the fall and winter, I observed some trees located across the street in front of my home. All of the trees in the area that were not evergreen plants had lost their leaves. I observed three trees directly in front of my home; they had lost a lot of leaves. However, there remained a few brown leaves still hanging on to the trees. They endured rain, hail, extreme cold and snowstorms. I watched and pondered their ability to endure these tremendous weather conditions. It is now the month of May and these few leaves are still holding on to the branches. There are also new leaves budding all around them. These leaves have endured the worst winter we have had in twenty years.

The Word of the Lord came to me every time I observed these trees from my window, that there are still a few names in Sardis who have not defiled their garments. It is very encouraging to know that there are still a few names in the church that are still holding on to truth despite the harsh conditions that have entered the church environment.

This book is not about a person selling his or her body in the physical sexual act for the gain of money. However, if any be involved in such physical sexual activity, whether for sale or not for sale, it is strongly recommended that you repent and turn away from such behaviour. There is only one sexual relationship that God established and sanctioned. This relationship is found in Genesis 2:24, "Therefore shall a man leave his father and his mother, and shall cleave unto his wife: and they shall be one flesh."

Any other sexual relationship outside of one man married to one woman is not in alignment with God's plan for human sexuality. God will judge all other relationships in which this sexual relationship is found. It does not matter which human authority legalized it, it will be judged by the Creator. Our bodies belong to God, and should not to be used for sexual sins, according to 1 Corinthians 6:19-20. It is God who sets the standard and boundary for human sexuality. Let the Word of God judge our sexual relationships. "Marriage is to be held in honor among all, and the marriage bed is to be undefiled; for fornicators and adulterers God will judge" (Hebrews 13:4).

You are holding this book in your hands for a purpose. It might be that none of these situations pertain to you. Hallelujah, there are a few in Sardis who have not defiled their garments, (Revelation 3:4). This book is written to set free, those who are entangled in these conditions. "If the Son therefore shall make you free, ye shall be free indeed" (St. John 8:36).

Should any of these be found in your life, receive correction and turn in repentance in the name of Jesus Christ. If none of these things pertain to you, let us join together in prayer for those who have been deceived into these things, that we will all have a heart of repentance. The Lord Jesus Christ spoke in St. Luke 9:56 that, He did not come to destroy men's life, but to save them. He came to reconcile the world to Himself, not to lay the charges of our sins to us, (2 Corinthians 5:19). All of us have sinned and come short of the glory of God, (Romans 3:23), that was why Jesus died. Jesus Christ paid the penalty for sin, so we do not have to continue in sin. Praise God, if any sin we have an advocate with the Father, the Lord Jesus Christ, according to 1 John 2:1. Thank you Father, Jesus nailed them all to the Cross and lives to make intercessions for us, (Hebrews 7:25). We don't have to continuously practice sin and bear them anymore. Jesus Christ came to change our lifestyle. Amen.

Based on a series of dreams, visions and revelations I received from our Lord, I decided to forward the information in a book. I didn't know how to relate to the Church what the Lord was showing me. I am not a preacher, so I knew I would not be called to preach on any pulpit. The word came to me to put the message in a book. While I was thinking on the idea, the thought came to me that John in Revelation was told to write to the churches in Asia about the things he saw, things that were and things that were to come. This is found in Revelation 1:19. Habakkuk was instructed to write the vision and make it plain. (Habakkuk 2:2.)

In this book, I have written the conditions of some of the assemblies that were revealed to me through the Holy Spirit. These dreams and admonitions are directly from the mind of the Spirit. Some of the warnings will be re-stated because of urgency. There will also be overlapping information of the various topics. The words in this book express the very feelings of our Saviour in regards to the condition of the church, which He purchased with His own blood. These words are not written in a "thus saith the Lord," tone. Nevertheless, it is written and understood as "these things saith the Spirit to the Church." Therefore, quoting the Lord's own word from the Holy Scripture in St. Mark 4:9, "And he said unto them, He that hath ears to hear, let him hear."

Upon receiving these dreams, I was the first one who was required to repent. This was not applied to others, while I walked away freely. I had to repent. I am blood-washed through water baptism, and a Holy Ghost-filled believer. I was a disciple in the Church (and still remain firm in the faith), which practices the precise biblical fundamentals directed by the apostles' teaching, as instructed by the Lord Jesus Christ, that we should observe. However, I was not excused from what the Lord Jesus Christ had to say to the churches. I had to repent all the way through writing this message.

I felt somewhat like Isaiah in the book of Isaiah 6, when he saw the Lord and His glory. Immediately, he realized he was a man of unclean lips and he was living among people with unclean lips. He was messed up. All along, Isaiah was prophesying, and he was doing great. Then he saw the Lord as He is. Isaiah repented and one of the angels took the live coal from the altar and placed it on his lips and told him his sins were forgiven and he was cleansed. I pray this is how everyone will see himself or herself. My hope for everyone is that the contents of this book will cause a holy stir in all who read it. Repent and cleanse us from all filthiness of our flesh and our spirit, as recorded in 2 Corinthians 7:1.

This book is going against the grain of modern conducts, which might leave some readers feeling extremely uncomfortable. This might be an unprecedented rebuke for the body of Christ that is written in a book. It might feel like a sharp prick or a double-edged sword that just sliced you, but receive it in the grace of God and search the scriptures. Jesus Christ is not willing that any should perish, but that all should come to repentance (2 Peter 3:9). Sometimes medicine has an unpleasant flavour, but it is good for us and makes us well again. This book is written for the purpose of, "Casting down imaginations, and every high thing that exalteth itself against the knowledge of God, and bringing into captivity every thought to the obedience of Christ." (2 Corinthians 10:5). It is not only written to expose the lies of Satan but to deliver people from the grips of his lies.

This book is for every denomination and for everyone who calls him or herself a Christian. It is also for those who have not received Jesus Christ and are of another religious sect. There is no guaranteed salvation besides Jesus Christ, for there is none other like Him. God's deliberate, ordained and implemented plan of salvation through the atonement of Jesus Christ is a guaranteed "one blood cleanses all," in every generation and nation under the sun. This book will help you find the way to salvation through Jesus Christ, so that you may obtain eternal life. It is not written to bash denominations or to bring condemnation but for edification. It is written to bring grace and to lead us solely to Jesus Christ. Therefore, I urge every leader, to whom the Gospel of Jesus Christ is entrusted, to preach Jesus Christ. Point the world to the Cross. St. Luke 12:48 says, "...For unto whomsoever much is given, of him shall be much required: and to whom men have committed much, of him they will ask the more."

This is heart-rending, soul-ripping, devil-destroying, Holy Ghost-restoring reading. The style and tone of language used in this book may not measure up to your particular or preferred style of communication. The presentation may not be politically or grammatically correct, but it is definitely Biblically correct. This was not written to expose political issues; therefore it was not written using political jargon. It was solely written to expose the lies of the devil and turn us completely back to God. If you do not intend to repent you can choose to put this book aside or you can choose to repent and turn to God. We still have the power to decide. 1 John 1:9 tells us that, "If we confess our sins, He is faithful and just to forgive us our sins, and to cleanse us from all unrighteousness." These words are written for you to respond to God and not to the messenger. I had to respond to the message and turn to Jesus Christ in repentance. Respond to God, Who sent the message. The Lord Jesus Christ is ready to forgive us of our sins. In Revelation 3:15, the Lord Jesus Christ says, "I know your works." Revelation 3:22 says, "He that hath an ear let him hear what the Spirit saith unto the churches."

I want everyone to know that Jesus Christ himself knows our works. He has already evaluated the works that we have performed and is somewhat against many of us. This is an urgent call to repentance.

1

Darkness in the Church

Dream

A church was having a convention. I entered the sanctuary. It was full of people. The pulpit was in the center of the sanctuary with the people seated around it in a circle. The large crowd of people were all dressed in white garments. The musicians were playing, the praise and worship team and the choir were singing along with the congregation. Everyone seemed to be spirited and worshipping. Then I noticed that the place was in total darkness. I could see them in the darkness but they did not notice that they were in darkness. I tried reaching my hands for a chair to hold on to as I walked because I couldn't see where I was going due to the gross darkness. I was afraid that I would trip and fall. I took my glasses off, but it was still dark. I used my hands to pry open my eyes and it was still dark. I watched as they read the Bible, collected the offering and the preacher preached in the darkness. I don't think they realized that they were in darkness. I *said, "Jesus, please turn on the light. Jesus, please turn on the light." I was begging and pleading for Jesus to turn on the light. I woke up out of the dream with the lights still off.*

I was perplexed by the scenery of the dream and sought the Lord for understanding. I asked the Lord, "Why was I asking Jesus to please turn on the light?" I heard in the spirit, "I am the Light and I'm not there, that's why there is no Light. The pulpit is the center of worship and not Me."

The light-less Church equals the Jesus-less church

Jesus Christ is the Light of the Church. Jesus states: "As long as I am in the world, I am the light of the world" (St. John 9:5). The people of God are the Church. He was not in the church, that's why there wasn't any light in the place. In other words, Jesus Christ was not in the people. He was not actively living in them. The saddest part is that the congregation had no idea that they were in darkness. If the Light is not in the church, it means the church has lost power and is operating in darkness. This revelation broke my heart.

Jesus said in St. Matthew 5:14, "Ye are the light of the world. A city that is set on a hill cannot be hid." How can sinners be saved, when they can't see the light?

Absence of light equals darkness. Church of the Living God, we are the light of the world. Shine as light and let the world see the light of Christ through us. Christ is the only way to God. Let our light lead the world to God. Saints of God, we are the only access the world has to Him.

Jesus Christ has been put out of the Church. Many assemblies have become "Ichabod," the glory has departed (1 Samuel 4:21). This occurred when there was war between Israel and the Philistines. The Philistines took the Ark of God. Eli's daughter-in-law gave birth to a son that same day and called his name Ichabod, saying, "The glory is departed from Israel." I encourage everyone to bring back Jesus Christ, the Glory and Light of the church, back into the church, and bring the Light to the world. It is only through the saints that the world will see Jesus Christ, the True Light.

Focal point of worship

"The pulpit in the center of the church is the focus of attention. It is the focus of the church. I am not their focus. I am the Light of the church. If I am not the center of worship, then I am not there. That is why there is no light in the church because I am the Light. They are doing everything that appears to represent me. They preach, read, worship, play music and even dress the part, but I am not the focus. The pulpit is the focus. I am not darkness. I am Light. It is not a physical light that is out, but the spiritual light. You prayed, "Jesus please turn on the light." I couldn't because I am the Light and I am not there."

How the church, His beloved, must break the heart of Jesus Christ! The church, that He gave His life for, has rejected him and they are doing things their own way. I wonder if He cries over the church like He wept at the grave of Lazarus. The center of worship is the pulpit. Glory and honour, praise and adoration are now offered to the pulpit. Worship is geared towards the pulpit and not to God. That is the why the church was seated around it in a circle. There is worship with the lips, but the hearts are far away from God.

It is no longer the ministry of Jesus Christ and the acts of the Holy Spirit. It has become, the ministry of John Doe and his great achievements. We are no longer workers together with Christ. Christ has become our part-time employee with a little praise benefits every now and then. The pulpit now seeks adoration of men. There seems to be a desperate need to be spoken highly of. Some have set themselves as idols in the assembly. They have paraded themselves around taking unto themselves the spirit of King Nebuchadnezzar who focused the spotlight on himself and not on the Most High God, who lives and reigns forever. Be careful of self-exaltation. King Nebuchadnezzar was driven from his kingdom and became homeless. He had the mind of a wild animal and lived with them in the fields. For seven years, king Nebuchadnezzar lost all human reasoning and lived the lifestyle of an animal. These animals accepted him with open paws. They graciously accommodated the king in their environment. The king roamed the open fields and rolled in the grass with them. His daily diet consisted of a fresh supply of grass. His bed was under the covering of trees and bushes. His nails grew as claws and his exposed skin grew hair like feathers. King Nebuchadnezzar's periodical baths were from the rain that fell from heaven. The facility for his bodily functions was in the wide-open fields, with nothing available to clean himself. His dialogues were with the wild animals, grunting gibberish, being made perfect in their dialect. If I understand the text correctly, he was insane or mad for seven years. In our modern day terminology, Nebuchadnezzar would be considered as having a mental break down or mental health issue. Daniel 4:30 tells us of the response of the king as he views the kingdom, "The king spake, and said, Is not this great Babylon, that I have built for the house of the kingdom by the might of my power, and for the honour of my majesty?"

Some angels of the church are now worshipping the works of their hands, and are persuading the saints to bow to their image and shrine. Many have refused to give God the glory that is rightfully His. The saint who gives them the flatteries they seek, are favoured with benefits. The ones who refuse to bow to their trumpet, to eat their meat and dance to their music are treated with disdain.

Repent and return the pulpit to God. Take your hands off God's glory. He will not share His glory with another. In Isaiah 42:8, God clearly stated this fact, "I am the LORD: that is my name: and my glory will I not give to another, neither my praise to graven images." Do not underestimate God's divine wrath. Give back the Lord Jesus Christ His pulpit before it is too late for you to return it. This is my plea to you as Daniel pleaded with the king in Daniel 4:27, "Therefore, O king, may my advice be pleasing to you: break away now from your sins by doing righteousness and from your iniquities by showing mercy to the poor, in case there may be a prolonging of your prosperity." NASB

2

Offering of Dead Foul Sacrifices to God

Dream

I was at a church service. This church sanctuary looked like a combination of several different churches. The service commenced with the Praise Team taking their position on the pulpit for worship. I was a member of the Praise Team. I noticed a coffin was placed at the altar, between the pulpit and the congregation. The pastor told the Praise Team to form a circle around the coffin, the altar and the pulpit, making one big circle, encompassing all three. The Praise Team formed the circle. One of the Praise Team members was told to open the coffin. The coffin was opened and there was an old dead man's partially decomposed body, all wrinkled and pale, in white clothing, lying in the coffin. There was a horrific odour coming from the coffin. The stench was nauseating. It reeked so badly that people were holding their noses and gasping. We were instructed to sing and praise God, as the coffin was open *with the odour. I said to them that we couldn't sing in here with this coffin and odour at the altar. However, no one listened to me. I removed myself from the Praise Team and went to the extreme back of the church and watched as the Pastor, Praise Team and the congregation offered exuberant worship in the stench. The stench was unbearable. Nevertheless, they proceeded with the worship service.*

Upon waking, I was greatly disturbed and pondered the dream and wondered what it could possibly mean. I went into prayer for understanding of the dream, and this was revealed to me:

Worship that is being offered to God

The church is offering to God, dead and unacceptable sacrifices that are foul and stink in His nostrils. The worship is polluted. It is not sweet savour. Instead, it is a nauseating and unbearable odour that is going up to God. This is our gift of worship to God. It is repulsive and horrendous before Him. This is how God sees it. Our worship is upsetting the stomach of God and makes Him want to vomit. According to Revelation 3:15-16, Jesus said, "I know thy works, that thou art neither cold nor hot: I would thou wert cold or hot. So then because thou art lukewarm, and neither cold nor hot, I will spue thee out of my mouth." We are offering dead, fleshy worship that is unclean and unacceptable. God will not tolerate this kind of worship in His presence. The Pastor was the one who gave instructions to the Praise Team to encircle the coffin, open it and to begin worship.

For the Pastors who are leading the congregations in polluted worship and are not teaching them to worship God in spirit and in truth, you are in trouble with God. God is vehemently angry. God is somewhat against you Pastors, who are leading the people astray. Worship has become entertainment. We come before God in worship, offering to him whatever we feel. We enter into worship with our malice, lies, backbiting, gossips, resentments, bitterness, grudges, adulteries, fornications, unforgiveness, covetousness, envy, strife and all kinds of sins that we get involved in. These sins were not repented of. We offer them to God in worship as if God must accept what we choose to give him. We come with the attitude, "Well, God this is what I have, take it or leave it, but that's all I am giving you." We are conveying the spirit of Cain in offering what we please. Where is the reverence in worship? Do we stop to recognize who God really is? It is God who sets the standards for worship.

What I saw at the altar in the dream was offensive. Which of us would appreciate someone coming into our home, and offering us foul and decomposed meat to eat? We would not eat it, but throw it out. We would not be pleased with the individual who purposely brought this into our home for our consumption. This has become our lifestyle of worship before God. Saints, some of us are offering meaningless, worthless, and useless sacrifices. Some are now worshiping at the "Altar of Self and Self-improvement." God is not pleased. Repent and offer to God sacrifices that are pleasing to him. Stop offering polluted lip service and give true heart service, the worship that is in spirit and truth to God. We are convinced that we are worshipping in spirit and in truth, but we never truly entered His presence.

Acceptable Worship

The word of God declares in Romans 12:1, "I BESEECH you therefore, brethren, by the mercies of God, that ye present your bodies a living sacrifice, holy, acceptable unto God, which is your reasonable service." Jesus said in St. John 4:23 & 24, "But the hour cometh, and now is, when the true worshippers shall worship the Father in spirit and in truth: for the Father seeketh such to worship him. God is a Spirit: and they that worship him must worship him in spirit and in truth." Our bodies are to be used to worship God. Staying away from sin and keeping ourselves pure and holy before God is true worship. Coming before God to worship with our lives packed with unrepented sin is not worshipping in spirit and in truth. To offer less than our Heavenly Father's requirement in worship, is unacceptable. True worship comes from a heart that is totally submitted to God. Our hearts are to be holy. This occurs through genuine repentance, and keeping our hearts pure by adhering to the Word of God. The Father is still seeking true worshippers.

3

Spirit of Slumber

Dream

I *went to a church convention. I sat in the church worshipping. The place was very dark and grey looking, like daytime in a building when the lights are out and windows are closed. It was time for "testimonies of praise." The moderator chose three ladies including me, to moderate that part of the service. I was very excited to do it. One of the ladies started singing a song as I got up from my seat. As my feet touched the pulpit I fell into a deep sleep. I knew I was asleep. I was still singing and could hear the congregation singing also. It was like I was drunk with sleep. I felt terrible that I was fast asleep on the pulpit while moderating the service. I tried waking up myself. This was difficult to do because the force of the sleep was so heavy. It took all my energy to wake myself up. I managed to bring myself to a seated position, open my eyes and realized that the other two ladies and the congregation were asleep. However, we were all still singing. Our singing was very faint and feeble like we were in a very drowsy state. It was like the sleep had paralyzed us. I tried waking up the other two ladies so that we could wake up the congregation and motivate them, but couldn't. I managed to stand up on my feet but was still very drowsy and shaky. I woke up out of the dream not being able to awake anyone.*

As I woke up I heard, "the church is sleeping. It is time to wake up out of sleep." I was very perplexed about the condition of the church as was revealed to me. An evil unclean spirit of slumber has taken over the church. It is while men slept, unaware that the enemy crept in and destroyed the lives of the saints. The spirit of slumber overcame me in the dream when my feet went on the pulpit. There is a spirit of slumber on the pulpit. The sad thing is, we are worshipping and don't realize that we are in a state of sleep. Saints, while we are sleeping the enemy is sowing seeds of discord, malice, hate, unforgiveness, bitterness, strife, gossip, slandering and such negative characteristics like these among us. This is causing us to be separated from God and from each other. The enemy is dividing and conquering the saints. Here is wisdom; a territory that is conquered does not remain unoccupied. The person who conquers it moves in and takes ownership quickly.

This spirit of slumber was transmitted to the saints in the congregation from the pulpit. Leaders, you are affecting the life and worship of the saints. Your actions have a direct influence and impact on the saints. Darkness in the church creates an atmosphere for the spirit of slumber to come into the church. This is neither light nor darkness. This reminded me of the lukewarm church in Laodicea, neither hot nor cold. Jesus told the lukewarm Laodicea church that because they were neither hot nor cold, He was going to spew them out of His mouth. Church, if we continue in this state of sleep, our light will be totally shut off. Many churches are sleeping. They are still doing everything that goes with protocol, but sleeping. They are in a deep spiritual sleep. These churches are physically active and performing everything that is on the agenda, but are in a spiritual coma. They feed the poor, but are asleep. They have their programs for the less fortunate, but are asleep. They evangelize to their community, but are asleep. They get involved in many community outreach and programs, but are asleep. Some have their prayer meetings, fasting services and Bible studies, but are asleep.

The spirit of slumber and darkness represent Satan's kingdom. It is Satan's kingdom that is being enhanced in a church that is sleeping and is in darkness. We are not of the darkness, which represents Satan and his activities. The dark greyness is sin. A state of holiness and righteousness has never created an atmosphere of greyness or darkness. It is sin that has put the church into a state of sleep. Where unrepented sin abides, the spirit of slumber dwells. Don't be drunk with sleep (sin), which is the work of the devil. Pastors, who are living a double life of worshipping God and serving the devil by committing sin, repent and turn to God. Walk away from the double lifestyle. Your sinful lifestyle is affecting the saints. Stop being double minded. Double mindedness causes us to be unstable in all our ways according to James 1:8. Such a person will not receive anything from the Lord. Be aware of the times in which we are living. "Do this, knowing the time, that it is already the hour for you to awaken from sleep; for now salvation is nearer to us than when we believed. The night is almost gone, and the day is near. Therefore let us lay aside the deeds of darkness and put on the armor of light. Let us behave properly as in the day, not in carousing and drunkenness, not in sexual promiscuity and sensuality, not in strife and jealousy. But put on the Lord Jesus Christ, and make no provision for the flesh in regard to its lusts" (Romans 13:11-14 NASB).

    Let the churches that are asleep wake up. We are not of the night but of the day. Do not continue in a state of slumber and allow the day of the Lord to come upon us unaware, according to 1 Thessalonians 5. Awake! Put on the robe of righteousness. Let us be dressed and ready for the coming of the Lord. Everyone who is asleep needs to wake up. It is the pure Word of God that is going to wake up those who are asleep. I strongly encourage those who are committed to preaching the Word of God, to preach the pure Word in truth.

4

Spirit of Envy

Dream

I went to a church service. I entered the sanctuary. The floor was muddy and had wet grass. There was no tile flooring. The chairs were old and some had no back. I searched for a place to sit where I could be comfortable, but could not find any. I saw a chair beside an old lady, so I went to sit beside her. The service was already in progress and everyone was having a spirited time. I wondered if they were uncomfortable in their seat because I was. They had the altar call and members went to the altar. The altar call turned into a time of praying for souls to receive the Holy Ghost. I watched as they prayed. The old lady sitting beside me said to me, "Do you see that pastor praying with that young man at the altar?" She pointed to the pastor she was referring to. I said, "Yes." She continued to say, "He is full of envy and he is transferring the spirit of envy to the young brothers in the church." I started screaming, "Jesus, Jesus, Jesus!" which woke me up.

If there is ever a time in Christianity when men have become envious it is now. There are some Pastors and members alike, envying and coveting what others possess. One Pastor envies another because of the size of the church building, membership of the congregation, and his accolades. This is the spirit of King Saul. King Saul was very envious of David's accomplishments, to the point of going after him to kill him. He chased him through countries as if David was a notorious murderer, armed and dangerous to society. There are saints envying each other's spouses, houses, material things, careers, ministries and so on. Each saint is trying to outdo the other. The church has become full of competitors and rivals all because of the spirit of envy. Saints of the Living God, be aware of the spirit of envy. Don't be influenced by this spirit.

Envy is an unclean spirit, who makes the individual feel a strong, emotional despise for another person because he or she does not have certain qualities or things that the other person has. The person with the spirit of envy will seek to have the same thing that the other person has or try to get something even better than the other person. The desire to acquire what the other person has is motivated by the spirit of envy. Envy is full of hate. A person who is influenced by the spirit of envy believes that the other person should not have certain things. This strong emotion causes one to have the intention to inflict harm or wish harm to come to the person that they despise. If harm should come to the person that this individual despises, the individual with the spirit of envy greatly rejoices and is extremely happy. This is not the spirit of God. Jacob's sons were prime example of being moved with envy. They sold their brother Joseph into slavery, because of his dreams. See Genesis 37 and Acts 7: 9. Where there is the spirit of envy, there will also be the spirits of resentment, covetousness, hate, greed, grudge, bitterness, malice and unforgiveness. "For where envying and strife is, there is confusion and every evil work" (James 3:16). It is God who weighs, examines and judges the content of the heart.

Envy and covetousness are neighbours, fuelled and prompted by jealousy. To covet is to have an excessive, passionate and wrongful desire for something that belongs to another person. Sometimes the person who has a covetous spirit will physically go after the other person's things and take it without permission. When this is done, the covetous person feels no compassion, nor remorse for the person he or she has harmed. Covetous individuals feel that they are in the right and that they are entitled to another person's things. We are not even to go to our neighbour's property and take a stone without that neighbour's permission. Remember the command of Exodus 20:17, "Thou shalt not covet thy neighbour's house, thou shalt not covet thy neighbour's wife, nor his manservant, nor his maidservant, nor his ox, nor his ass, nor any thing that is thy neighbour's." Jealousy is a strong negative emotion of possession, or, wanting to possess what is your own or something that belongs to someone else. This emotion can engulf and consume the person like a vehement flame burning on the inside causing anger, resentment, and the need to retaliate or take negative action.

The spirit of envy is all about, the "Kingdom of Me." This is the era of the self-seeking and self-serving kingdom. The Self-seeking Kingdom is about God blessing me and nobody else. The Self-seeking Kingdom says to Jesus, "Let me sit on your right hand and my son on your left hand, and nobody else. The Self-seeking Kingdom feels that this is my ministry that I built, with my name and no one else will ever get his or her name on it.

Spiritual transmission

Many Christians are not aware that evil spirits are transferable. Being unknowledgeable about this fact, a naive Christian is at risk of having unclean spirits transfer to their life. These unclean spirits will influence and damage their life greatly. Whatever spirit the Pastor is of, that is what he will transfer to the congregation. The Pastor, who speaks from a heart of envy, releases the spirit of envy on the congregation. If he speaks from a place of compassion and love, compassion and love are released on the congregation. A Pastor might be telling the congregation to love, while speaking from a heart of hate. Some weak saints in the congregation might find themselves hating. While the Pastor is wondering why, after teaching on the subject of love so many Sundays, there are people who still have trouble loving. The saints are trying to love but don't have the strength to love, because the message came from a heart full of hate. Check your spirit. The weak saints who are not strong in the Holy Spirit will receive the spirit from where the leader is operating. Those who do not know how to discern in the spirit will be affected because they do not know how to guard their spirit. For example, a person who takes a glass that is dirty and pours some juice in it, risks all the filth in the glass will mix with the juice and go straight into their tummy. At times the person may experience sickness and sometimes death may occur because germs were in the glass. When a preacher preaches, and his or her heart is not clean, as the Word is released from an unclean heart, souls are at risk. Repent and be converted.

5

Off Course, Out of Range

Dream

I took a chartered bus, going to a specific mall in the area where I reside. The name of the mall was written on the front of the bus. This trip to the mall was about a twenty-minute drive and was not far from my neighbourhood. It was a warm bright summer day. I noticed after travelling on the bus for a while that I did not recognize any of the places we were passing. It suddenly became dark. I heard the driver announce, "Next stop, New York City." I said to the person sitting beside me "I thought we were going to the mall." She also thought the same. I thought about how it would take eight hours to reach New York and another eight hours to get back. I did not have time to waste. I got up from my seat, went to the driver and asked him where exactly we were going. He said, "This bus is an express to New York City." I told him I want to get off the bus because the original sign said we were going to the Mall. He told me that he was not allowed to let anyone off the bus *until we reach the destination. I insisted that he drop me off because I am not going to New York. I told him "this bus was way out of range, and off course from where they advertised that it was going." I persisted and he eventually stopped the bus, let me off in the middle of the road in a dark deserted place and told me that I can cross the street and get a bus going back in the other direction. I wasn't dressed for the conditions of the weather that this bus had taken us. It was a warm summer's day when I got on the bus. I had sandals on my feet and no coat on. It was a cold winter night with snow on the ground when I stepped off the bus. Fortunately, I couldn't feel the cold neither did my feet get wet or frozen from the snow I had to step in. The bus drove away and I crossed the street alone, to get to the next bus stop. I woke up and the thought came to me forcefully "some churches are off course and heading in a direction far from God."*

This is heart breaking. Many assemblies started out in the right direction but are now heading in opposite direction from where God had intended for them to go. I live in the north. New York is south of where I live. This dream was given to show that some churches are heading down instead of up, farther and farther away from God. This was totally off course and out of range from the word of God. The weather in the beginning of the dream, where I boarded the bus, was summer and I was dressed appropriately. The place where I got off the bus was dark, cold and full of snow. These were two totally different climate conditions. Many hearts have become cold and callous and some church conditions are the same.

The driver stated that he was not allowed to let anyone off the bus. Satan had ensured that his trip is an express trip. No one is allowed off. It is the trip to hell. This journey was dark and cold. We were going where we did not intend to go. Satan will take us farther than we could ever imagine that we would go, and ensure that there is no way for us return. His trip is so fast and steep, leaving us no control to stop and get off. He has one destiny for us and that is to take us to a place of enslavement and utter destruction. The people on the bus did not want to go to New York. They wanted to go to the mall a few blocks down the road. However, none had the courage or the strength to get up and get off the bus. I am not stating that New York is a place of hell. New York has many saved people. I also have saved friends in New York. So please do not misunderstand what is being said to the church. It is a representation and not the actual place. God chose to use New York in this dream for His own purpose. I believe it is to show the extremity of where we should be to where we are heading. The mall represents a specific, confined small spot that is manageable, with few stores in it that are attainable to go through in a few hours. New York City speaks of the enormity of the location and inconceivable things to do in an enormous degree to one's pleasure, day and night. It speaks of extravagance and indulgence. It would take a long time to enjoy everything that the heart desires. Satan's trip is exhausting. He will present to us everything we desire that is evil and fulfill it for us. Then when we are fully engaged in our desire he locks us in with no way out. Don't be deceived. The enemy of our soul will always come in an ingenious way that looks pleasing and comfortable to catch and obliterate us. He sets up his demolition parties waiting to completely eliminate us in total.

    I strongly recommend to everyone, insist on your soul following hard after God. Pursue the Word of God with all diligence. Take a stand for your own soul and the soul you pastor. Do not allow anyone to lead you down a path that is not the path of godliness. I lovingly encourage leaders to listen attentively to God and not to emotions, traditions and unproven doctrines. I caringly encourage followers to know who you are following. Everyone be wise and redeem the time. Know that we are living in evil times and evil is becoming more extreme as we approach the end of the age. Understand that deception is increasing to enormous levels, as is eminent in the scriptures. Search the scripture, and turn your life around into the direction of God, if you are one that is off course and out of range.

One day I was traveling to a place I had not been before. I input the address into my GPS and followed the instructions of the GPS. I did not write down the directions because I had confidence in the GPS that it would accurately get me there. My journey began and it was going well. I made all the right turns and was very pleased. What a wonderful invention, I thought to myself. I decided that I knew a few main roads that I could take to get to the main spot that I knew and then I would follow the GPS direction. I heard the GPS several times rerouting me back to its instructions, but I insisted that I knew a different way. Then I heard from the GPS "signal lost, searching for signal." I continued driving, waiting to hear that the GPS has signal for me to continue my journey. No such luck. I was so glad that I had the phone number of the place where I was going. I made a stop and called the place, told them exactly where I was and received the rest of the directions to get there. This was to my own detriment, not following directives, being confident that I know the way, at least part of it.

The thought came expressly to me that many have lost the signal that connects them to Christ. Disturbances have interfered with the relationship. Many outside interferences have occurred to disable the relationship. The love of many has already gone cold. There is no connection to Christ. The sad thing is that many are not aware that they do not have a connection to God. If we are not connected to Christ we cannot complete the journey. Jesus Christ is the only way to God. Some have already moved out of their place in God. I peacefully implore those who have lost connection and their direction with God, seek Him with all your heart and turn your life back to Him. Obey His words. Take heed to your own way. Get back into fellowship with Him. He is patiently waiting for you.

6

Satanic Symbol

Dream

I was in a building that looked like a school portable. There were other people in there with me. We were preparing and setting up food for a function. In the middle of setting up a gentleman, who appeared to know me well and whom I was familiar with, said, "Sonia come take a look at this." He handed me a symbol that was attached to a keychain. I took it and looked at the symbol. It was the satanic symbol of baphomet and under it was written "The Church of Jesus Christ." I said to the man, "I know in my spirit that the pastor was involved in evil but did not know it had entered the church to this extent; that secretly it has become a worship of idols." I cried out, "The church, Jesus, the church!" I held the symbol in my right hand and fell on my knees and continued to cry; "The church, the church!" I then fell prostrate on the floor and continued to cry "The church, the church! Jesus, help the church." I realized that we were in serious *trouble because unknowingly to us what was being presented to us was not what was actually happening. The gentleman at this time lay on my back as if to protect me while I was interceding for the church. The people around me started asking "Sonia, what is it? What do you have in your hand? I did not respond to them but continued to conceal the keychain in my hand and intercede for the church. I did not want them to see the reality of what they were actually worshipping. I was troubled in my spirit to show them that they were being deceived. Someone came in and said that we were called to come to the main auditorium to pray. I got up and went through the door with the others. I told them that I have a key to lock the door. I had a key that was not attached to the keychain. I used it and locked the door. Someone came back and said, "We can stay in the portable where we are and pray." I unlocked the door and we went back inside. I woke up.*

I remained in my bed astonished, and pondered the dream. I closed my eyes praying to God in regards to what I had just received. As I lay there praying, the following vision was what appeared to me.

I was transported to the first room of a church building. This room was extremely dark. I saw the brightness of a man standing in the entrance of the open door. His face shone with light. All around where He stood was light. He was clothed in a long white robe with a golden sash around His waist. I could not look in his face because of the light that was radiating from His face. His total being was light. He did not speak. I kept my eyes pierced on Him as he slowly faded away. I could no longer see Him. I tried very hard to get the light and the man back in the door but there was only darkness. The darkness inside the church was equal to the darkness that was outside of the church.

I opened my eyes and became perplexed over what I saw. Why was a demonic symbol located where the cross should be? Why was "The Church of Jesus Christ," located under a satanic symbol? Why was I pleading "the church, the church?" What caused Jesus Christ to fade away? Why was there no light in the church? Why was inside the room as dark as outside? I wanted to know if both the dream and the vision were connected. I began to ask God to show me the meaning of the dream and the vision.

The man who gave me the keychain was an angel, who was sent to show me what was taking place in some of the churches worldwide. He was also sent to cover and protect me. The key that I used to lock and unlock the door represents legal access, entry and right. Praise God that this key was not attached to the keychain. The man, with his countenance of light and garment of white, was our Saviour, the Lord Jesus

Christ. The darkness represents Satan's kingdom and sin.

Many assemblies are using the name of Jesus and have become the assemblies of Satan in disguise. They have become a haven for demons. They started out well serving Jesus Christ but soon gone after the way of Balaam the prophet as recorded in Revelation 2:14, "But I have a few things against thee, because thou hast there them that hold doctrine of Balaam, who taught Balac to cast a stumbling block before the children of Israel, to eat things offered unto idols, and to commit fornication."

In their hour of temptation, when the devil approached them and showed them a small piece of the kingdoms of the world that he would give to them if they would bow down worship and accommodate him in the church; they did not rebuke the tempter but accepted his proposal. The devil has enticed them to keep their religion, still profess Jesus but not in His entirety. The dragon knows that half-truth and half lie is a lie and will never gain them eternal life. His deal with them is to continue with their services but dilute the Word so that it is not concentrated on Jesus Christ. Now, many have sold their soul and the assembly to the devil for personal gain. They are preaching contrary to the Word of God by compromising and tailoring God's

Word to accommodate the world's system, which is a demonic system.

Many have sold out to the enemy. They have become devil worshippers. They kept the name "The Church of Jesus Christ," but have pledged allegiance to Satan. They have become unfruitful workers of darkness doing shameful things in secret. Ephesians 5:11-12, tells us of their deeds. The name is used as a cover up so that they are not easily identified. Many are deceived into thinking that they can bear the name of Jesus Christ, produce fruits of iniquity and still be saved. This is a strategically planned and calculated lie of the devil. They carry out the assignments of Satan. They have become idol worshippers. Many of the saints are sitting down in these assemblies and are not aware that they are in an idolatry assembly that uses the name of Jesus Christ for a front. Inwardly, they have given themselves over to demons and profess outwardly, Jesus Christ.

Some have already exchanged the Cross of Christ for the glamour and glitter of the world that Satan gave them, of which they accredited to God. They loved fame and fortune so the lying dragon has given to them their heart's lust and has chained many. They believe that they still have Jesus dwelling with them but don't realize that Jesus Christ has faded away out of their midst, as they have brought in more darkness into the church. Many assemblies now resemble the world in its totality. There is no difference between the darkness that is in some assemblies and the darkness in Satan's kingdom. The sin that is in the church is equal to the sin that is in the world. The darkness is sin and iniquity. I encourage everyone to awake to righteousness. Measure up your lifestyle with the Word of God and not the dictates of the world.

Take a good look in the Word of God and take a look at your assemble and your own life. Does your work resemble God or does it resemble Satan? Which kingdom are you truly living in and operating from? Are you producing the fruit of the Holy Spirit or the works of the flesh? Who are you seated beside in the spirit realm? Is it with Jesus in heavenly places or with Satan in the kingdom of darkness? Are you serving the Prince of Peace or the prince of the power of the air? Who is your King? Is Jesus Christ your king or is Beelzebub your king? Who is Lord of all in your life and assemble? Your fruits will speak for you as to who is your lord. "Beware of the false prophets, who come to you in sheep's clothing, but inwardly are ravenous wolves. You will know them by their fruits. Grapes are not gathered from thorn bushes or figs from thistles, are they?" (St. Matthew 7:15-16) NASB. Have you sold out to material things? Have you sold out solely to Jesus Christ? Whose mandate are you carrying out? Is it the mandate of the Cross? Is Baphomet your mandate? Are you truly the church of Jesus Christ or the assembly of Satan? You can't serve two masters. Choose today whom you will serve. Don't let Jesus Christ fade away from you.

Those who have called themselves saints, what communion has the light of Jesus Christ with darkness? Light and darkness can never cohabitate. Why are you joining and yoking yourself with devils? Does righteousness have fellowship with unrighteousness? Does Christ have any communion with devil? How is it that Jesus Christ does not have any relationship with the devil and you find it possible to have one with devils? Does the temple of Christ have any agreement with idols? How is it that so many have found a way to come into agreement with idols? Since we are the temple of the living Christ, who is dwelling in you? Who is walking in you? Who is your God? Who do you really belong to? The Word of God in 2 Corinthians 6:14-17 expressively exhorted us to come out from among these unclean things and don't touch them. Let us separate ourselves from these things and Christ will receive us. Jesus Christ is the Light. If He is gone then darkness is what we will inherit. Put away the idolatry.

Come out from among the unclean things and choose Jesus Christ. "He that saith, I know him and keepeth not his commandments, is a liar, and the truth is not in him. But whoso keepeth his word, in him verily is the love of God perfected: hereby know we that we are in him. He that saith he abideth in him ought himself also so to walk, even as he walked." (1 John 2:4-6).

7

Laodicean Whores in Today's Church

As I was waking up early one morning to pray, I was having a conversation with someone in my sleep. The person was speaking about the Church practicing spiritual whoredom. It was said with such disgust and scorn. I thought about what I heard. The conversation was so real, I thought that someone was in the room with me but there was no one. I realized that I was hearing this in the spirit. I felt sick. I thought, "God, this is degrading. This is a horrible thing to say." I felt ashamed, because I knew that somewhere in that statement, I was included. For a few days I could not bring myself to think about what I heard. I felt weakness in my feet. These words had such a crushing reproachful and shameful sound. It had such an impact on me. I didn't want those words in my ears or in my thoughts.

On hearing this conversation, I decided that I did not want to pursue or get an understanding from the

Lord of the reason for it, because it sounded very serious. So I decided that I would not seek the Lord regarding it. I didn't want to know its meaning or deal with it. I thought that if I could block it out of my mind, it would go away and it won't matter because I didn't know what it meant. It began to haunt me. It was like someone who I couldn't see was following me wherever I went.

I went to visit a church service a few days later and the Pastor was teaching on "Spiritual whoredom in the church." I thought about the chances of this happening. The same week I had the opportunity to hear another Pastor speaking at different place on "The church going into spiritual harlotry." I was totally in awe and realized that there was no getting away from it. I knew that it was time to expose the whoredom in the church. The Lord was speaking to me and I needed to stop and listen intensively and attentively to hear what he wanted me to know.

I did not want to end up like the prophet Jonah, who ran away from the mission God sent him on, but not from the eyes of God. Jonah went the opposite direction, ending up in the belly of a great fish that God had provided as a private express transportation specifically designed for him. The great fish, taking him three days and three nights journey through the harsh conditions of its belly and turbulences of the sea, deposited him right in the place God had commissioned him to go, Nineveh. The event of this story is found in the book of Jonah. I decided to listen attentively.

Many Christians claim to know God, and that they have the Truth. They boast of being filled with the Holy Ghost with the evidence of speaking in tongues, and have understanding of the one true God. They profess that they are washed in the blood of Jesus Christ and bear His name. Yet some have totally denied the ways and practices of God. Their hearts are far from God. Some have committed whoredom. Some have sold themselves and some have given away themselves for free. These have committed whoredom with the world and with devils. Many have become like the children of Israel, in their migration from Egypt to the Promised Land. They were at times, trying to find a way back into Egypt to be enslaved and eat onion and garlic. So many of the churches have gone back to eat the husk of the world and be entangled with sin. The true proverb has fallen on many in 2 Peter 2:22, "But it is happened unto them according to the true proverb, the dog is turned to his own vomit again; and the sow that was washed to her wallowing in the mire."

They have been found in Satan's bed. They have given their hearts to another. They have listened to seducing spirits. Like Samson, who found himself in Delilah's bed, so the Lord has uncovered them in Satan's bed. The devil has stripped them of their strength, integrity and identity. Satan has plucked out their eyes so that they cannot see the Truth. All they have is a form of truth but not TRUTH. They are pulling down false teachings on themselves and others because of their loss of sight, causing spiritual impairment. They have gone back to entangle themselves with the yoke of bondage and do not realize that they are quickly disintegrating. These have given birth to children after their own kind, weak, without integrity, and no identity. Their children do not know God. They profess they know God and that Jesus Christ is their Lord, but they don't obey Him or do His will. Many in the church and in the body of Christ have become Satan's prostitutes and are found sleeping and carousing with devils and the world. This is how the title of the book was birthed.

8

Empty Baptismal Pool

Vision

I was in a church service and as I was sitting there, worshipping, I was taken away in the spirit for about five seconds. I saw a baptismal pool before me. I looked in the pool. It didn't have any water in it. It appeared abandoned, parched, dried and have some debris at the bottom of it. I heard, "This is barrenness and a deserted pool."

I visited a church service and picked up a bulletin. I read the advertisements. To my surprise, the next water baptism will take place in the next six months. This was offered only two times per year. They do have classes for those who would like to follow Jesus. This was being offered as a choice to those who wanted to follow him through baptism. I didn't realize that there were options in baptism. To baptise or not to baptise, this seems to be by choice. What will happen to those souls if Jesus Christ comes to take his church out of the world within the six months? What will happen to the individual who dies before the six months? Water baptism is not frequent or necessary in some church circles anymore. The church is going through a drought for souls. Some churches are experiencing a harvest of souls while some are fruitless.

Water baptism is an immediate response

Jesus Christ commanded the disciples to go and baptize the nations in St. Matthew 28:18-20, **"And Jesus came and spake unto them, saying, all power is given unto me in heaven and in earth. Go ye therefore, and teach all nations, baptizing them in the name of the Father, and of the Son, and of the Holy Ghost: Teaching them to observe all things whatsoever I have commanded you: and, lo, I am with you alway, even unto the end of the world. Amen."** It is noted in St John 3:22, 23 & 26, while on the earth, Jesus witness and sanctioned the disciples baptizing others who came to follow Him, **"After these things came Jesus and his disciples unto the land of Judaea; and there he tarried with them, and baptized. And John also was baptizing in Aenon near to Salim, because there was much water there: and they came and were baptized. And they came unto John and said unto him, Rabbi, he that was with thee beyond Jordan, to whom thou barest witness, behold, the same baptizeth, and all men come to him." Understand that Jesus trained them in baptism in the resources of St. John 4:1-2, "WHEN therefore the Lord knew how the Pharisees had heard that Jesus made and baptized more disciples than John, (Though Jesus himself baptized not, but his disciples.)"

The Lord Jesus Christ was baptized by John, who did not find himself worthy to baptize Jesus in the book of St. Matthew 3:13-17, "Then cometh Jesus from Galilee to Jordan unto John, to be baptized of him. But John forbad him, saying, I have need to be baptized of thee, and comest thou to me? And Jesus answering said unto him, Suffer it to be so now: for thus it becometh us to fulfil all righteousness, Then he suffered him. And Jesus, when he was baptized, went up straightway out of the water, and, lo, the heavens were opened unto him and he saw the spirit of God descending like a dove, and lighting upon him: And lo a voice from heaven, saying, This is my beloved Son, in whom I am well pleased."

Upon hearing the gospel for the first time on the day of Pentecost, after the Holy Spirit fell on the disciples, the multitude wanted to know what they needed to do for them to be saved. The answer is recorded in the Book of Acts 2:37-39, "Now when they heard this, they were pricked in their heart, and said unto Peter and to the rest of the apostles, Men and brethren, what shall we do? Then Peter said unto them, Repent, and be baptized every one of you in the name of Jesus Christ for the remission of sins, and ye shall receive the gift of the Holy Ghost. For the promise is unto you, and to your children, and to all that are afar off, even as many as the Lord our God shall call." Immediately after Peter preached Christ to the Jews (who were gathered in Jerusalem for the Feast of Pentecost), explaining to them what they needed to do to be saved, three thousand souls who heard the Word were convicted and baptized the same day, not a few days after. Jesus Christ trained Peter and the disciples in baptism. The water baptism event of Acts 2 was not the first baptism they had performed. This was a continuation of what Jesus Christ had trained them to do. The disciples were baptizing people before Acts 2:38. Now, Jesus was gone and they knew exactly what to do and how to do it. Therefore, they executed the command by Jesus Christ in the manner that they were trained. Acts 2:41, "Then they that gladly received his word were baptized: and the same day there were added unto them about three thousand souls."

The apostle, Peter did not speak a word of error when he told the multitude to repent and be baptized everyone in the name of Jesus Christ for the remission of your sins and you shall receive the gift of the Holy Ghost." Peter was taught by Jesus Christ Himself and carried out the command of Jesus Christ to the letter. Peter understood the full deity of Christ. Peter and the other apostles never changed anything that Jesus Christ commanded them. We were admonished in Colossians 3:17, "And whatever you do in word or deed, do all in the name of the Lord Jesus, giving thanks to God and the Father by him."

According, to St. John 3:22 and 4:1-2, before the crucifixion and resurrection, Jesus was there when His disciples were baptizing people. The Bible said that Jesus Himself did not baptize any but His disciples did the baptizing. If they were baptizing in error, He would have corrected them. Jesus Christ did not hide anything from His disciples. Obviously, the disciples continued to perform water baptism as they did when they were with Jesus. Jesus is known for rebuking the disciples for wrong actions and wrong motives. Jesus Christ would have corrected this important institution, if the disciples were administering it outside of what Jesus had commanded them.

Philip was told by the angel of the Lord to go to Gaza. He went and met the Ethiopian eunuch who was reading the book of the prophet Isaiah. After Philip explained the word clearly to him, they came to a place where there was water, and the eunuch was baptized there. Acts 8:36-38 tell us of the reaction of the eunuch when Philip preached to him about Jesus Christ, "And as they went on their way, they came unto a certain water: and the eunuch said, See, here is water; what doth hinder me to be baptized? And Philip said, if thou believest with all thine heart, thou mayest, and he answered and said, I believe that Jesus Christ is the Son of God. And he commanded the chariot to stand still: and they went down both into the water, both Philip and the eunuch; and he baptized him." Again in Acts 8, Philip went down to Samaria and preached Christ unto the Samaritans. Many of the Samaritans believed and were baptized according to Acts 8:14-16, "Now when the apostles which were at Jerusalem heard that Samaria had received the word of God, they sent unto them Peter and John: Who, when they were come down, prayed for them that they might receive the Holy Ghost: (For as yet he was fallen upon none of them: only they were baptized in the name of the Lord Jesus.)"

Paul and Silas were in prison for casting out the spirit of divination from a young slave girl and for preaching Jesus. The Bible tells us that at midnight they prayed and sang praises to God. This resulted in a great earthquake that opened every prison door and broke every prisoner's chains. The jailer, thinking that all of the prisoners had escaped, was ready to kill himself. Paul called out to him that he should not hurt himself because they were all accounted for. After Paul explained Christ to the jailer, he was immediately baptized. Let the Word speak for itself in Acts 16:30-33, "And brought them out, and said, Sirs, what must I do to be saved? And they said, Believe on the Lord Jesus Christ, and thou shalt be saved, and thy house. And they spake unto him the word of the Lord and to all that were in his house. And he took them the same hour of the night, and washed their stripes; and was baptized, he and all his, straightway." Their baptism was not extended to another time. In other words, upon hearing the Word of God they were baptized right away. Believing on the Lord Jesus Christ needs to be followed with repentance and water baptism. Believing alone doesn't give a person access to the Kingdom of God. Even the devils are believers in one God. James 2:19 informs us that, "Thou believest that there is one God; thou doest well: the devils also believe, and tremble." In St. Matthew 8:29 the devils identified Jesus Christ as the Son of God. Does believing in God make the devils a Christian? Does their belief save them and give them access to enter the kingdom of God? It is written in the Bible that the devils believe, so where does this put them? Are they not believers? We know from the Word of God that, all devils will be cast in the lake of fire. Therefore, believing in Jesus Christ requires that we obey what He has commanded us to do. We show that we believe by the way we carry out His teachings. We live what we believe. Water baptism (full immersion) is a must in entering the kingdom of God. To sprinkle water, as a form of baptism, on someone is not being fully submerged in water. Sprinkling of water for baptism is not recorded in the Word of God. Let's baptize as it is written in the Word. St. Mark 16:15-16 stated, "And he said unto them, Go ye into all the world, and preach the gospel to every creature. He that believeth and is baptized shall be saved; but he that believeth not shall be damned." In the event that one hears the Word of God and says he or she believes and refrains from baptism, does not believe in His Word.

Let's take a look at the apostle Paul in the Book of Acts 9. Saul, who made havoc of the church of the living God, was on his way to Damascus to put in prison, anyone who called on the name of Jesus. Jesus Christ met him on the way. The light of Jesus Christ shone on him, threw him off his horse and blinded his eyes. He cried out to God saying, "Who are you, Lord?" Jesus replied, "I am Jesus who you are persecuting." Saul inquired of Jesus what he would like him to do. Jesus told him to continue to Damascus and he will be told what to do. Jesus Christ spoke to the prophet, Ananias, regarding Saul and what he needed to do for Saul. Ananias went to Saul as the Lord had commanded him and baptized him in Acts 9:18, "And immediately there fell from his eyes as it had been scales: and he received sight forthwith, and arose, and was baptized."

In the Book of Acts 10, we read the account of Cornelius, the Gentile who was praying in his house. He had a vision of an angel who came to him with a message. The angel told Cornelius that his prayers and giving had come up to God as a memorial. The angel instructed Cornelius that he should send men to Joppa to get Peter and Peter would tell him what he ought to do. Cornelius sent men as he was told and got Peter. After Cornelius related his experience with the angel, Peter preached Jesus Christ unto all who were gathered at Cornelius's house. The Holy Ghost fell on all of them while Peter was still speaking as noted in Acts 10:47-48, "Can any man forbid water, that these should not be baptized, which have received the Holy Ghost as well as we? And he commanded them to be baptized in the name of the Lord. Then prayed they him to tarry certain days."

Why are we forbidding water? Why are people being taught to just believe in their heart, raise their right hand and repeat a prayer and they are now saved? Acts 4:12

declares that salvation is in Jesus; "Neither is there salvation in any other; for there is none other name under heaven given among men, whereby we must be saved." Why are we not commanding the nations to repent? Men and brethren, we must observe and do all that the Lord commanded the apostles. The apostles have instructed us in the ways of God. Go back to the Word of God. We are instructed to observe and carry out to the letter all things that the Lord Jesus Christ has commanded the apostles. Water baptism is to be administered to someone who is conscious of his or her sin and has chosen to repent.

A baby is not conscious of sin and therefore cannot repent and turn away from sin. Water sprinkling on a baby is not baptism and is not recorded in the Word of God. The act of sprinkling babies with water was not commanded by Jesus Christ and was not practiced by the apostles. Water baptism requires full immersion of the individual into the water, from feet to head. In the all powerful, supernatural plan of God, when someone goes down in the water in the name of Jesus Christ, in obedience to the Word of God, the blood of Jesus Christ is immediately applied to the sins and the sins of the person are washed away. In other words, those sins are extinct, never to re-appear anymore. The person will never have to give an account for those sins forever.

Water baptism is an act of obedience to Jesus Christ. If we can't follow Jesus Christ instructions in the initial step, how are we going to follow Him all the way?

Water baptism, a requirement of the Kingdom of God

Nicodemus came to Jesus Christ in St. John 3. Jesus Christ was the one who initiated the conversation that a man must be born again. We are not exactly sure what the purpose for Nicodemus going to Jesus by night was; the scripture did not get into it. Jesus Christ told him that a man must be born again to see the Kingdom of God. Upon hearing this Nicodemus, wanted to know how a man can be born again when he is old. "Jesus answered and said unto him, Verily, verily, I say unto thee, Except a man be born again, he cannot see the kingdom of God. Nicodemus saith unto him, How can a man be born when he is old? Can he enter the second time into his mother's womb, and be born? Jesus answered, Verily, verily, I say unto thee, Except a man be born of water and of the Spirit, he cannot enter into the Kingdom of God. That which is born of the flesh is flesh; and that which is born of the Spirit is spirit" (St. John 3:3-6). Being "born again" was instituted by Jesus Christ and not by the will of man. It is impossible for one to enter the Kingdom of God without being "born again" in the specific way that Jesus Christ has laid out for man. It is with great sadness that I say this to those who have not followed Jesus in water and the spirit, you have not yet entered the Kingdom of God.

One day, I put one of my dishcloths in hot water to soak, so that whatever was in it may come out. Nothing came out of the cloth. The thought came to me to try it again, only this time to add detergent to the water. I did, and immediately the water started changing colour. A few minutes later I took a look at it and the water was brown. The solution in the water made the difference. It cleansed the cloth from all the dirt that was in it and the cloth became clean. The water of itself did very little for the cloth. This thought came strongly to me: So are those who do not go down in baptism in the blood of the Lamb. Those who do not put on Christ will still remain in their sins. They have not been cleansed. It is the blood of Jesus Christ that cleanses from sin.

There is only one way into the Kingdom of God as stated in the Word of God. The way into the Kingdom of God is being born of the water (baptized) and of the Spirit (Holy Ghost). All must come through the blood of Jesus Christ, which was shed at Calvary. There is no other way written in the Word of God for a man to enter the Kingdom of God. Neither is there any other command given by our Lord Jesus Christ for man to enter the Kingdom of God. Don't be lazy. Search the scriptures for yourself. On the day of the Lord's judgement of each of us, as we stand before God, we will be responsible for the Word of God. Even if someone taught us a false doctrine, we are responsible for taking the initiative in searching the Word of God to see if what is being told to us is truth.

There will be no excuse for lack of knowledge of the Word of God. "I did not know" is not an excuse. If man can say ignorance is no excuse for the law, how much more for the Word of God that He said man must live by. Take responsibility for the feeding of your soul. Do not rely on someone every Sunday morning to spoon feed you and take in everything they give you whether good or evil. Some have already taken in poisonous teachings into their soul. Get up and daily learn to feed on the Word of God for yourself. Ask God for understanding of His Word and He will abundantly give it to you. "My people are destroyed for lack of knowledge: because you have rejected knowledge, I will also reject you from being My priest. Since you have forgotten the law of your God, I also will forget your children" (Hosea 4:6 NASB).

I am aware that the context of this word in Hosea was written to the Israelites. Surely, this also applies in this context. They had rejected the knowledge of God, and God said I would also reject you that you should be no priest to me and I don't want your children that you have produced either. When we don't know the Word of God, we won't know what His laws require of us. We see the results of the nations that forget God. The results are never a happy one. A Christian without knowledge of the Word of God is heading for destruction. Some are being raised as lazy self-seeking Christians, who do not have any appetite to study the Word for themselves, becoming a generation who do not know God. Be an active doer of the Word of God. Take ownership for your soul.

I realized that some churches are truly in a drought. Many baptismal pools have not been in use for months, some years. The assembly appears to be growing but only with new members migrating from one assembly to another. There is a famine in some assemblies. Repent and return to God in water baptism.

"Sinners prayer" for Salvation

Satan has erected his own monuments of being saved, by tricking souls into believing that if they follow his disguised way, they will be saved. He is aggressively recruiting souls to join him in the Lake of Fire. God has given the church power to incapacitate, dismantle and annihilate demonic reasoning and operations. Since Jesus

Christ Himself became obedient in baptism, how is it that we have become disobedient in baptism? The Word of God is here to set free, all who are bound by the doctrine of just pray the "sinner's prayer" for salvation.

Some assemblies have excluded water baptism from salvation and have incorporated the "sinner's prayer," which replaces water baptism. I want to say it clearly: Water baptism is not optional. In their doctrine, water baptism is viewed as not essential to salvation. This is totally in error. There is no record in the Word of God regarding the "sinners' prayer" for salvation, given by Jesus Christ. Neither was it taught by the disciples who were told to teach the nations to observe all things that Jesus Christ had commanded them. Jesus Christ himself was baptized and said that it was necessary to fulfil all righteousness. Why are we omitting baptism?

Water baptism is essential and is a righteous act that is commanded by Jesus Christ Himself. Since all power is given to the Lord Jesus Christ in heaven and on earth and He has commanded water baptism, what power then has any man on earth, to change God's command? By which power will such a person enter the Kingdom of God? Saints of the Most High God, return to the living Word of God. Those who are practicing the "sinner's prayer" as entrance to salvation, you have been deceived and you are leading the congregation and yourself in error. The "sinner's prayer" alone is insufficient. Water baptism must accompany repentance. Search the scriptures.

Many of these wrong teachings were concocted many centuries ago and have been passed on through the generations as truth. These have been innocently accepted as gospel truth. I have learned that, if you have learned something wrong, you will teach the wrong you have learned to others, because that is how you know it. You cannot afford to continue to hide behind these wrong teachings any longer because they do not lead to eternal life.

Jeremiah 23:1 states, "Woe be unto the pastors that destroy and scatter the sheep of my pasture! Saith the LORD." There is a greater condemnation to those who are pastors who destroy the people with wrong doctrines and cause them to go astray. Pastors, your punishment will be greater than the flocks. We cannot modify salvation to accommodate people with itching ears, who want to enter heaven on their terms. Not one person will enter heaven on his or her terms, only through the prescribed way given by Jesus Christ. Let Romans 6:3-5 liberate you, "Know ye not, that so many of us as were baptized into Jesus Christ were baptized into his death? Therefore we are buried with him by baptism into death: that like as Christ was raised up from the dead by the glory of the Father, even so we also should walk in newness of life. For if we have been planted together in the likeness of his death, we shall be also in the likeness of his resurrection."

Precious ones, were you baptised into Jesus Christ? If you repeat the "sinner's prayer" and you believe that you are now saved, you are not. If you have not yet been baptized into Jesus Christ, you are not buried with Jesus Christ by baptism into death. Therefore, you have not been raised to walk in newness of life. You are still in the domain of death. You have not been translated from the kingdom of darkness. You are still in your sins, they have not been removed. You are still groping around in darkness. It is impossible for anyone to have newness of life without water baptism. Yes, water baptism was instituted by Jesus Christ and still stands. Jesus Christ has not changed it for our generation. Jesus said in St. Luke 6:46, "And why call me, Lord, Lord, and do not the things which I say?" St. John 14:15 states, "If you love me, keep my commandments," and St. John 15:14, "You are my friends, if you do whatever I command you."

The apostle Peter warns us in 2 Peter 2:1-2, "But there were false prophets also among the people, even as there shall be false teachers among you, who privily shall bring in damnable heresies, even denying the Lord that bought them, and bring upon themselves swift destruction. And many shall follow their pernicious ways; by reason of whom the way of truth shall be evil spoken of." These are the days that false teachers are unleashed in the earth. They present their doctrines in clever and cunning ways, which eventually lead their followers unexpectedly to ruins. These false teachings or as the Bible calls them "doctrines of devils" are like sink holes appearing as solid ground, but waiting to collapse and engulf its occupants. When we twist the scriptures, it only results in our destruction. God does not have various ways to be born again in different generations or centuries. God has only one way for every generation in every century, and that is through Jesus Christ. Any other institution outside of what Jesus Christ has instituted is null and void. Let's deliver you from this error.

There is only one way to God and that is through Jesus Christ. If you try another way, the Bible declares who you are like as written in St. John 10:1, "Verily, verily, I say unto you, He that entereth not by the door into the sheepfold, but climbeth up some other way, the same is a thief and a robber." If we don't go through the door (Jesus Christ), then we are climbing up some other way to get into the kingdom and it is impossible. The Word of God says such persons are thieves and robbers in St. John 10:9-10, "I am the door: by me if any man enter in, he shall be saved, and shall go in and out, and find pasture. The thief cometh not, but for to steal, and to kill, and to destroy: I am come that they might have life, and that they might have it more abundantly." Jesus Christ declared it plainly that He is the door and He has come to give abundant life. Satan is a thief and he comes to steal, kill and destroy. Come through Jesus Christ and you will have eternal life. Jesus said, "My sheep hear my voice, and I know them, and they follow me: and I give unto them eternal life; and they shall never perish, neither shall any man pluck them out of my hand," (St. John 10:27-28).

It is commanded of us to pray. For a person who has not accepted Jesus Christ as his or her Lord and Saviour, saying a prayer of repentance and confession is good, but incomplete without baptism. This must be followed by water baptism in Jesus Christ in order for salvation to become effective in that person's life.

Salvation through mouth confession

Another error common among some who handle the Word of God is the belief that if you just confess with your mouth to the Lord Jesus Christ and believe in your heart you will be saved, even if the person is not baptized. This is a misunderstanding of the Word of

God. It actually applies to saints who had already gone the way of water baptism. This is found in Romans 10:8-10. There must be the evidence that this person has repented and has been identified with Jesus. Please note that all the epistles that were written by the apostles were addressed to the saints, or to individuals who were already redeemed, exhorting them how to live now that they are in Christ. The epistles were not written to sinners who were not in covenant with God through the blood of Jesus Christ. The book of Acts of the Apostles, gives many accounts, details and experiences of how many souls came into the kingdom; and this is the exact direction in which we should continue in carrying out the mission and commission of Jesus Christ. The Word of God was preached; the people heard the Word, they repented of their sins, were baptized in Jesus Christ, received the Holy Ghost and continued in the Apostles teachings.

After the death, burial and resurrection of Jesus Christ, It is only through the blood that we enter the Kingdom. The blood of Jesus Christ must be applied to every sinner that will enter into the Kingdom of Christ. Without shedding of blood there is no remission of sins. See Hebrews 9:22. The sinner must be purified with blood because it is only the blood of Jesus Christ that removes sin. The sin issue must be taken care of before entering the Kingdom of God. The covenant of His blood is applied when we are immersed in water. We go down in His name because it is His blood that cleanses the sin away. We are identifying with Christ in baptism, which means we have accepted and are identifying with His shed blood and His death. We cannot enter paradise, after the death, burial and resurrection of Jesus' complete work, except through baptism. No sinners' prayer will give anyone eternal life. Just opening one's mouth and confessing Jesus Christ and believing that Jesus rose from the death, without going the way prescribed by God for salvation, will not grant anyone eternal life. The blood of Jesus Christ must be applied. Mouth confession alone is not the key to salvation. Stop trying to use this as a key to enter the kingdom. It is the wrong key and it will not open the door. This wrong key of confessing with your mouth to the Lord Jesus Christ and repeating the "Sinners' Prayer" without baptism will only open the gate of hell for your soul. Every sin must be washed in the "blood of the Lamb" through water baptism.

"Once saved, always saved"

Satan is a master liar and deceiver. He is the father of lies. Any time he speaks it is guaranteed to be a lie. He has propagated his lies to the church and the church received it as truth. There is no truth in him. St. John 8:44 described his attributes and the attributes of his children; "Ye are of your father the devil, and the lusts of your father ye will do. He was a murderer from the beginning, and abode not in the truth, because there is no truth in him. When he speaketh a lie, he speaketh of his own: for he is a liar, and the father of it." He does not know how to speak the truth for the truth is not in him. The same way he permeated the Garden of Eden and fed Eve with lies; he is doing the same with many who are supposed to know truth. Eve knew the truth. She could eat of all trees in the garden including the tree of life, except the tree of the knowledge of good and of evil. Satan twists the truth with a little lie and many accept it as truth. If it is part truth and part lie, it is a lie and never the truth. Satan is still telling people the same lies in different situation that they can remain in the Garden of Eden even if they eat of the tree that God has strictly forbidden them to not eat of. He tells people that they can remain saved and go to heaven if they continue to sin. He tells them that they shall live and be as wise as God. Stop falling for the lies of the devil. He told Eve in the Garden of Eden that she shall not surely die. She obeyed the serpent, ate of the forbidden fruit, gave her husband the lie to eat, both died, received God's swift expected judgement, and was cast out of the Garden of

Eden forever. They were told that the day they eat of the fruit of that specific tree God had strictly forbid them to eat, they would surely die. There was no one or two more chances given to them. It was a one-time act followed by an immediate judgement and punishment. See Genesis 2.

"Once saved always saved" teaching, has infiltrated the church. This teaching proclaims that your salvation is eternal and you never lose it. If you believe this teaching, it is not true. You have believed a lie. You have been deceived. Satan is using the same deceptive lie he used on Eve to destroy you. This is a blatant lie of Satan. He is telling people and whole congregations that God will permit them to enter heaven with sin. If we turn away from following the Lord Jesus Christ, how then can we be saved? This is a very strong delusion. This is a doctrine that encourages people to live a very sinful life. One who has been washed in the blood of the Lamb cannot live a wilful, habitual life in sin, remain saved and go to heaven with Jesus Christ without turning from that sinful life. Yes, the finished work of Christ is indeed complete. One cannot add to it or take away from it. The destiny of man's fate hangs on his adherence to salvation. Man still has a choice, after he has accepted Jesus Christ, to discontinue his relationship with Him.

This teaching claims that once you have believed on the Lord Jesus Christ and you have accepted him as your Lord and Saviour, then you are forever saved and you cannot lose your salvation. This doctrine implies that no matter how you sin, you will always be saved. You can return from following Jesus, go back to the elements of the world, continue the same old lifestyle you once lived, and you are still guaranteed to be in heaven with Jesus Christ, when He comes back for the church. Lies, Lies, Lies. Has Satan so veiled our eyes that we cannot see? Only those who do the will of God can live forever in eternal life. "And the world passeth away, and the lust thereof: but he that doeth the will of God abideth for ever" (1 John 2:17).

Continuing in sin is not doing the will of the Father. We cannot continue to live any kind of life and enter heaven. We can only enter heaven by the exact requirements of Jesus Christ. Stop trying to use God's grace as a license to sin. Salvation is to deliver man from sin and is not a certification to sin as we please. God's grace does not give us permission to transgress God's laws. God's grace brings liberty from sin and not liberty to sin. For those who live and believe these lies, the "second death" has power over you. Unfortunately, the conclusion of this for those who have believed this teaching and do not repent is at the white throne judgement of God, when they hear depart from me I did not know you. There will be no second chance to get it right.

Eternal life is a gift from God. God gives eternal life to those who obey Him. Sin has wages attached to it. Sin's wages is death. Eternal death is what one receives for sin. Stop allowing that Old Serpent to slither into the congregation and teach fables. If you and I do not live according to God's holiness we will inherit the Lake of Fire. This Lake of Fire that Jesus has prepared is a real place. It is as real as the waters of Noah's time. It is not a representation of a time of suffering. The "Lake of Fire" is a real "Lake of Fire." This Lake of Fire is forever. There is no end to it. Satan, his angels and all who are not found written in the Lamb's Book of Life will be cast into the Lake of Fire, which burns forever. "And the devil that deceived them was cast into the lake of fire and brimstone, where the beast and the false prophet are, and shall be tormented day and night for ever and ever. And I saw a great white throne, and him that sat on it from whose face the earth and the heaven fled away, and there was found no place for them. And I saw the dead, small and great, stand before God and the books were opened, and another book was opened, which is the book of life: and the dead were judged out of those things which were written in the books, according to their works. And the sea gave up the dead, which were in it, and death and hell delivered up the dead, which were in them: and they were judged every man according to their works. And death and hell were cast into the lake of fire. This is the second death. And whosoever was not found written in the book of life was cast into the lake of fire" (Revelation 20:10-15). Is this place worth your soul? Knowing the terror of God, I admonish you to turn away from false doctrines and turn to the God of Truth.

In Revelation 19:20, the beast and false prophet that were deceived by Satan into doing miracles and causing the people to take the mark of the beast and worship the image were the first ones to be cast into the Lake of Fire. One thousand years later, they are still in the Lake of Fire being tormented with fire, waiting for Satan, all devils and the rest of the disobedient ones to join them forever and ever. Is this place really worth living an ungodly life for? The Lake of Fire is the final home for Satan, his angel and all who were not found written in the Lamb's Book of Life. This is such a horrible place. I strongly encourage everyone to get right with God. Regrettably, wide is the gate and broad is the way that leads to destruction and narrow is the gate and way that leads to life. Only few walk the narrow way; the majority take the broad way that leads to destruction. See St. Matthew 7:13-14.

Dearly beloved, death is not the end of us. Death is the beginning of real life. After death comes the judgement. The Bible states that death and hell were cast in the lake of fire. See Revelation 20:14. When one dies and did not accept Jesus Christ, he or she goes immediately to a place called "hell," a temporary place until the time of their judgement. This is a place of unimaginable, unbearable, but real horrific torment, torture, pain, anguish, thirst, hunger, sleeplessness; worms etc. Hell is a place, where those who found themselves there, are tortured with inconceivable torments. "The wicked shall be turned into hell, and all the nations that forget God." (Psalm 9:17).

The majority of souls will be cast into hell, because of the choice that was made not to repent from sin and turn to Christ. Unfortunately, for most people this earth will be all the paradise they will ever experience. Pause, think about that and let it sink into your soul. There is no party going on in hell; if there is a party, only the demons are having it, while they are joyous that they have deceived another soul. There is no relief in hell. Hell is a real place and it is happening right now to the departed souls. Souls are there this very minute, trying to escape but there is no exit door. They are trapped. After the Judgement of God, they will be cast in the Lake of Fire forever. I know this is hard to believe but believe it or not, it is so. Saints and loved ones, a living person cannot repent for a dead person soul to be saved. A dead person cannot repent of his or her sins. The living cannot save the dead neither can the dead save the living. There is no special place for the dead to wait for a loved one to pray them out of and pray them into heaven. This teaching is a myth. There is no remission of sin in hell. Each of us has an appointment with death and the judgement that we must keep. See Hebrews 9:27.

The message of the Cross is not preached in hell, it is preached on the earth. The time of Grace is now, while we are alive and can make a decision of where we will spend eternity. Each day we live we are making a decision as to where we will spend eternity. We will be with Christ enjoying eternal life or with Satan in eternal damnation in the Lake of Fire. In death, it is too late to make a decision. The decision has already been made on earth. In every deed done, we are making a decision. In every word spoken, we are making a decision. In every action performed, we are making a decision. Choose wisely. For those who have already departed this life and Jesus Christ was indeed their Lord and Saviour, they are in Paradise. Knowing the terror of God, I strongly admonish everyone let us not take chances with our one soul. St Luke 16:19-31 relates the story of Lazarus and the rich man who both died and each went to their destination as they had decided on earth. The decision is made here on earth, while we are alive and not when we are dead. It is recorded that the rich man begged Abraham to send Lazarus back to earth to warn his five brothers not to come to this place of torment. Abraham told him to let them hear the laws and the prophets. This incident of Lazarus and the rich man was happening in the present and not in the future. Again there is no word preach in the grave or in hell. Only on earth do we have the opportunity to hear the Word of God and change our ways. At the death of each of us, our body goes to the grave and our soul immediately goes to hell or to paradise. Waiting period or grace period is not available in death. These are options during our lives.

Let's deliver you from this lie of Satan. It is the Word of God that sets us free. Romans 6:1-3,7,8,12,13,16,18,19,20,21 & 23 the question is asked, "What shall we say then? Shall we continue in sin, that grace may abound? God forbid. How shall we, that are dead to sin, live any longer therein... know ye not, that so many of us as were baptized into Jesus Christ were baptized into his death?... For he that is dead is freed from sin... Now if we be dead with Christ, we believe that we shall also live with him... Let not sin therefore reign in your mortal body, that ye should obey it in the lusts thereof... Neither yield ye your members as instruments of unrighteousness unto sin: but yield yourselves unto God, as those that are alive from the dead, and your member as instruments of righteousness unto God...Know ye not, that to whom ye yield yourselves servants to obey, his servants ye are to whom ye obey; whether of sin unto death, or of obedience unto righteousness?...Being then made free from sin, ye became the servants of righteousness...I speak after the manner of men because of the infirmity of your flesh: for as ye have yielded your members servants to uncleanness and to iniquity unto iniquity; even so now yield your members servants to righteousness unto holiness...For when ye were the servants of sin, ye were free from righteousness...For the wages of sin is death; but the gift of God is eternal life through Jesus Christ our Lord." I encourage everyone to please read the entire chapter of Romans 6.

Beloved, have you been baptized into Jesus Christ's death? What evidence do you have that you have been freed from sin? The only verification that we have that we have been freed from sin is when we have been baptized into Jesus Christ. Let it be known that, if we have not died with Christ, we will not be living with Christ. Continuing a lifestyle in sin is evident that sin still has power over us. We have not died to sin and we are not free, according to the Word of God. Whoever we submit our bodies to, righteousness or sin that is who we are servants to. If we surrender to righteousness we are the servants of God. If we surrender to sin we are the servants of Satan. We cannot continue to practice sin and be servants of God. We can't serve two masters. Since the wages of sin is death, how then can one who is habitually practicing sin remain "once saved always saved?" Eternal death is the reward for sin.

Saints and friends, there is no eternal life given to anyone who lives a sinful life, only eternal death. How can someone who did not finish his or her course receive eternal life as a reward? How can a person, living a lifestyle of unrepented sins, hear "well done?" Are we living to hear "well done" in sin or "well done" in righteousness? In the world system when a person registers for a course in school and he or she did not complete the course, do they get rewarded? They get an "incomplete, or fail." Only those, who successfully complete the course gets rewarded with a certificate. In a race, an athlete does not get a gold medal for an incomplete race. He gets the gold medal for being the first person in the race to complete it. How is it that we are telling people that they will be rewarded with eternal life for not completing their journey with Jesus Christ? We thank God that in this journey of Christianity everyone who completes this race gets rewarded with eternal life. There is no first or last place in this journey.

I pray that no one reaches this point, "For in the case of those who have once been enlightened and have tasted of the heavenly gift and have been made partakers of the Holy Spirit, and have tasted the good word of God and the powers of the age to come, and then have fallen away, it is impossible to renew them again to repentance since they again crucify to themselves the Son of God and put Him to open shame. For the ground that drinks the rain which often falls on it and brings forth vegetation useful to those for whose sake it is also tilled, receives a blessing from God; but if it yields thorns and thistles, it is worthless and close to being cursed, and it ends up being burned" (Hebrews 6:4-8 NASB). We cannot taste of the good things of God and go back to the deplorable things of the world and remain saved. If we refuse to bear fruits of righteousness and continually bear fruits of unrighteousness (sin), we will be cut off. Thorns and thistles were not created the day that God created all plants. They came on the earth as a curse, resulting from Adams disobedience. See Genesis 3:17-19. Thorns and thistles are a burden and painful. They are a hindrance and useless to man. They do not produce anything that can sustain life. They are only good to be burned. Sin is seen as thorn and thistle. At the gathering of God's harvest where ever thorns and thistles (sin) are found, they will be cast in the fire. Hebrews 10:26-27 tells us, "For if we go on sinning wilfully after receiving the knowledge of the truth, there no longer remains a sacrifice for sins, but a terrifying expectation of judgment and the fury of a fire which will consume the adversaries" NASB.

Let us refrain from following these false teachings. Pull away from all of it. Understand the times we are living in. Many false Christ and false teachers, messengers of Satan are in the world propagating lies. Remember the Words of Jesus in St. Matthew 7:21-23, "Not everyone who says to Me, 'Lord, Lord,' will enter the kingdom of heaven, but he who does the will of My Father who is in heaven will enter. Many will say to Me on that day, 'Lord, Lord did we not prophesy in Your name, and in Your name perform many miracles?' And then I will declare to them, 'I never knew you; depart from Me, you who practice lawlessness" NASB.

If you have obeyed Jesus Christ through repentance, water baptism and receiving of the Holy Ghost, and you have found yourself living habitually in sin, repent, turn away from it and allow Jesus Christ to help you daily in overcoming the besetting sins. If you have subscribed to the teaching of "Once saved, always saved salvation" unsubscribe and get your soul saved. Be aware of the snares of the devil. These false teaching are set to entangle us and to eventually destroy us. If you are a pastor who preaches this doctrine, put away the pride from your heart; love your soul and the congregation you pastor enough to put it aside, repent and turn whole heartedly to God. Be delivered in Jesus name from this doctrine of devils. It is not God's will for us to live a sinful life. Let us endure the journey to the end and we will be saved. St. Matthew 24:11-13, "Many false prophets will arise and will mislead many. Because lawlessness is increased, most people's love will grow cold. But the one who endures to the end, he will be saved" NASB.

We have been warned in the Word of God. Therefore, we must take heed because we have no excuse. Let us endure sound doctrine to the end. To be saved in the end, we have got to stay saved. Whether saved till we depart this life through death or saved when Jesus comes to take the church home. Remember to rightly divide the Word of Truth. The epistles were letters written to the saints who were already "born again." Appropriate to the church, what is designated to the church. Appropriate to the world that which applies to the world. My prayer is that the Lord Jesus Christ will give us all understanding.

Relationship through the blood

God created man to have relationship and take pleasure in Him. "You art worthy, O Lord, to receive glory and honour and power: for thou hast created all things, and for thy pleasure they are and were created" (Revelation 4:11). It is recorded in Genesis that God would come in the cool of the day to communicate with Adam. God is a God of relationship. The sin of man had caused damaged to the relationship. God cannot dwell where sin lives. God is holy. God made a way back into fellowship with Him through the blood of Jesus Christ. It is through the blood of Jesus Christ that we have an entrance to God. Without the blood we cannot enter His Holy presence. Being buried with Jesus Christ into baptism is a public declaration that we have accepted the shed blood of Jesus Christ in washing away our sins. We are now accepted into relationship with God and are in covenant with Him. We are now at peace with God.

The angels were created to serve. "Bless the Lord, ye his angels, that excel in strength, that do his commandments, hearkening unto the voice of his word" (Psalm 103:20). They are seen in various scriptures carrying out God's command. Hebrews 1:7 & 14 states, "And of the angels he saith, who maketh his angels spirits, and his ministers a flame of fire. Are they not all ministering spirits, sent forth to minister for them who shall be heirs of salvation?" All things were created for God, for distinct purpose. The earth was created for man. Angels were created to serve God and the saints. Angels, even though they were created greater than man, their purpose is to serve and protect. God has crowned man with glory and honour and not the angels. "Thou madest him a little lower than the angels; thou crownedst him with glory and honour, and didst set him over the works of thy hands" (Hebrews 2:7). God has honoured man by setting man over the things He created on the earth. God did not give any of the angels this honour. Saints, we were created by God for God. This is the greatest love story ever. We are called the sons of God and the bride of Christ. What a marvellous blessing! We cannot afford to be seduced by demonic teachings. Let's get it right as God intended.

Jesus Christ did not shed one drop of blood for the angels that sinned, including Lucifer. They were automatically thrown out of Heaven from the presence of God. There is no remission of sin for them. They will never again have any fellowship with God; neither will they ever be reinstated to their former position or habitation. These will be cast into the Lake of Fire. They do not have a hope. Those who are deceived by these cast away, fearful, rejected by God, angels and follow their way, will also be joining them in the lake that burns with brimstone and fire. Where water is not available to quench their thirst and the worms that fed on and do not die. On the other hand, God has made provision for us who accept the remedy for sin through the shed blood of Christ. Our reward will be life eternal with Jesus Christ. He has gone to prepare a place for all of us. Soon we will be with Him forever. Amen.

A time for the word

Have you ever been in a service where the preacher was preaching, and you couldn't hear the words, because the music was blaring over the word? Everyone is up on his or her feet shouting and having a good time but barely hearing what's being said. This is a distraction that the enemy has put in the church. The music causes you to become spirited and at the same time blocks the Word because it is too loud, so that the Word does not enter the heart of man. Weakness occurs in the body, when the Word of God is blocked from entering the ears and the heart has not received the Word. The spirited man needs the nutrients of the Word. It appears that some preachers need the high playing music to inspire them and arouse the congregation. When we are living in the spirit we don't need the music to bring fire to the Word. Many saints leave the service feeling pumped and motivated but not remembering what was said because they did not hear. This type of excitement is very short lived. It is the Word of God that waters the soul and causes us to repent and turn to God. The Word of God is spirit and life. "It is the spirit that quickeneth; the flesh profiteth nothing: the words that I speak unto you, they are spirit and they are life" (St. John 6:63).

The genuine, unadulterated Word of God is not very common. We get good preaching, but starved for life giving, soul stirring producing Word. Sermons are neatly tailored, full of words, and spirited. Preaching has become an art for some. They know when to arouse the crowd to stand and get spirited. They bring in their theatrical, dramatic methods to stimulate and pump up the people. It is time for those who minister the Word to get back to lying on their faces before God, to receive His Word of spirit and life to feed the congregation. Preachers, it's time to get before God and get a fresh Word. God knows what each congregation needs. Stop feeding the congregation on regurgitated food you downloaded from another source. Downloaded word is to aid in building you up and not to be copied and pasted.

Working at the altar has become deafening. The altar worker has to be yelling in the ear of the individual. The music is blasting over the singers. The altar workers can't hear, and the person being ministered to can't hear. The trick of the enemy is to block the soul from receiving the Word and the invitation of the Saviour. If the soul can't hear the Word, no life will be produced. Faith comes by hearing the Word of God. It is hearing of the Word that causes faith to germinate in the soul and allows them to accept Christ. If an individual can't hear the Word, there will be no faith and no life. Romans 10:16-17 states, "But they have not all obeyed the gospel. For Esaias saith, Lord, who hath believed our report? So then faith cometh by hearing, and hearing by the word of God."

We have very skilful and talented musicians and we have benefited greatly from this ministry. We appreciate all of our musicians. God is the creator of music. Music is a part of the ministry and a great part of worship. Thank the Lord. Let everything be done in decency and in order. There is a time for the music and a time for the Word. There is a time to play thunderous music. God is a God of order, not of disorder. As mighty and powerful as God is, He did not create everything in one day. Imagine if God had spoken everything to come into existence all at once. Some things were created from water and some from the earth. The almighty Creator did everything in a timely and organized manner. There is a time for the Word and there is a time for the music. Let not another soul be distracted from the Word of God because of the thunderous playing of music. Souls need to hear the Word of God. They need to repent and turn to Jesus Christ. The church is where they hear the requirement for salvation. Give them the opportunity to hear. Each soul is precious.

9

Field of Rotten Veggies

Dream

I went to a church to visit. I sat in the back row. The service went on and I began to feel very uneasy. I said to myself," why did I come here? I shouldn't have come here!" I got up to leave and noticed outside of the back of the church was a field that looked like it had vegetables in it. I recognized two people that I knew in the field. They were gathering the vegetables. I went to the field to tell them goodbye. I saw that there were corns there. So I asked for one corn. I was told that they were all paid for already so I couldn't get any. The corns had worms in them and parts of them were rotten. She proceeded to get some tomatoes for me. They were all rotten and eaten out. Some were dripping brown slimy liquid. She managed to find two of the best in the field, which were slightly rotten with a little part of them eaten. She put them in a bag and gave them to me. I took the bag, said thank you and goodbye. I *thought within myself as I walked away that I will have to throw these tomatoes away for they are not good to eat. I woke up.*

I considered the dream and asked for the understanding. The veggies represent what is being produced and given as food to the people of God. The field looks great but what is being produced is full of worms and rottenness, not suitable for consumption. There was not one vegetable found that was edible.

Producing feeble saints

Remember the words written in Revelation 22:18-19, "I testify to everyone who hears the words of the prophecy of this book: if anyone adds to them, God will add to him the plagues which are written in this book; and if anyone takes away from the words of the book of this prophecy, God will take away his part from the tree of life and from the holy city, which are written in this book" NASB. This was written in regards to the revelation of Jesus Christ in the book of Revelation and is relevant to the whole counsel of God. We are not given permission to add or subtract from the Word of God.

I was speaking to a custodian one day as he picked up the regular garbage and the recycle papers. Apparently, a little food was thrown in the recycle bin and the custodian had to throw the whole thing out. I asked him why he didn't just thrown the food part in the regular garbage and put the rest in the recycle bin. He said it was contaminated with the food so the whole thing had to be thrown out. I said to him that it is just a small amount of food, and I am sure it did not touch all the papers, just the ones that were on top. His reply was that has long as something else gets in, the whole thing is classified as garbage and cannot be considered recyclable material.

The Word is being mixed with the things of the world. Anything that is concentrated in its original form and gets contaminated with something else is no longer pure and does not do what it was supposed to do in its full strength. What is being produced or given is not effective because it is tampered with. Adding and taking away from the Word of God is tampering with the Word. Tampering with "the evidence" in the natural world is cause for imprisonment and can cause someone who is innocent to go to prison. Some have altered the Word of God, causing damage to the flock of God. They become unhealthy, malnourished, sick, feeble, lifeless, and weak saints. They have no substance to keep them fit in their daily walk with God. Many are falling at the slightest of problems. They can't take any pressure. They have no Word in them to combat the lies of the devil.

They fall prey to him daily because there is no Word of Life in them to keep them. They have no root and substance. They are not equipped to resist the wicked one. God is not going to resist the devil for us. We are instructed to resist the devil and he will flee. We resist the devil with the Word that we have in us. James 4:7-8, "Submit yourselves therefore to God. Resist the devil, and he will flee from you. Draw nigh to God, and he will draw nigh to you. Cleanse your hands, ye sinners; and purify your hearts, ye double minded." God has given us His pure Word to resist Satan. Preach the pure Word of God. To resist the devil requires that we know and speak the Word of God to him. Mixed up Word cannot chase the adversary away. Many Christians are resisting God, while drawing near and submitting to the devil, because there is no "Spirit and life Word" in them.

Itching ears saints

Many saints cannot endure sound doctrine because they have given themselves to seducing spirits, listening to doctrines of devils, having itching ears, always wanting to hear a new preacher and a positive word. Ceaselessly, they look for someone to prophesy in the name of the Lord, to tell them great things are coming in their lives, and to affirm them. 2 Timothy 4:3-4, "For the time will come when they will not endure sound doctrine; but wanting to have their ears tickled, they will accumulate for themselves teachers in accordance to their own desires, and will turn away their ears from the truth and will turn aside to myths." NASB

In the natural, an itch is very irritating. The only relief is to constantly scratch in order to soothe the irritation, which is only a temporary relief. Another form of relief is to get prescribed medication to remedy the cause of the itch. A person who has been described as having "itching ears" means that this individual constantly seeks to hear something that is in agreement with his or her lifestyle that is not in alignment with the pure Word of God. This ungodly lifestyle is an irritant because it is in opposition to the designed lifestyle that God has instituted for mankind. The individual relentlessly seeks out teachings to satisfy the itch or to support the lifestyle in order to soothe the guilty feelings. The only remedy to permanently cure the irritant is the Word of God. That irritant is called "sin." The blood of Jesus Christ was shed to get rid of that irritant so that we can all live a guilt-free life. Don't allow your conscience to be smeared with a hot iron disallowing you from responding to the call of God.

We live in an age where we want to live according to our own rules and wishes, and so we seek out teachers who are in agreement with our philosophy. We reject the truth and chase after fables and myths. We have bought into the deception of the enemy. Many "tellers" are now telling people what they want to hear. They invented their own prophecies in the imagination of their minds and say, "Thus saith the Lord…" The one being prophesied to goes home and things get worse and worse. Someone told them they were going to be healed and they died. Stop inventing and telling lies. If the Lord didn't speak it, don't speak it. Sometimes it is our wish and intention for them to be healed. I am not discrediting prophecy because there are true prophecies that have come through by real prophets. Let the prophets prophesy as God uses them. As surely as there are true prophets, there are also false prophets. If you are not a prophet, don't tell lie on God. Tell them your prayer for them is that everything will work out for them that, they be healed, get the job, marriage will work out, etc. But don't tell them thus saith God, when God has not spoken. When we do that, we are giving them lies to eat. This is a rottenness that will make saints weak and discouraged, and at times cause them to doubt God. Some of these prophecies are full of worms and rottenness. These prophecies are only fit to be cast in the burning Lake of Fire. Stop polluting the saints with devil-engineered food. Saints, refuse from eating demonic food. Feed on the pure Word of God. Let God's Word fill your entire being.

Return to the Holy Spirit

I was praying one day for those who were not filled with the Holy Ghost. I was carrying a burden in my heart for them. While I was praying, something was revealed to me. The church has a lot of social activities and game nights for most age groups. This is designed to keep everyone socially connected and to let everyone have a sense of belonging. This is all great for everyone. However, in some assemblies it has become far more important than prayer meetings, fasting services, time of waiting with individuals who need the Holy Ghost and times of Bible studies. Some churches don't even have corporate prayer meetings and Bible studies. Those who do have services experience poor attendance, especially with prayer meetings and fasting services. The majority of this time is spent with the preacher talking to the people, and a minimum amount of time talking to God.

There is very little time, if any at all, spent with those who need the Holy Ghost. The Word of God declares in Romans 8:8-9: "So then they that are in the flesh cannot please God. But ye are not in the flesh, but in the Spirit, if so be that the Spirit of God dwell in you. Now if any man have not the Spirit of Christ, he is none of his."

Some converts are sitting in the church and don't know about the Holy Ghost. They don't know that they need to receive the Holy Ghost with the evidence of speaking in tongues. Speaking in tongues is the proof that you have received the Holy Ghost. Yes, Holy Ghost tongues are for these days, just like it was for the Apostles days. It is the promise of God, as Peter declared on the day of Pentecost, for you, your children and your children's children, and for as many that are as far off even as many as the Lord our God shall call. That's for us in the 21st century. The Holy Ghost is not to come. He is here. Let's get back to the commission of Jesus Christ. The Holy Ghost to the saints was a promise of Jesus Christ as He communed with the disciples. Jesus said that He would send the Comforter. The Holy Ghost is given by God and not by man. Saints, be not deceived. Understand the strategies of the enemy. Satan is not going to come in a harsh, rough way to us when his intent is to deceive and bring into captivity. He will seduce us with enticing words, telling us how good it is. He will tell us this will be great for the congregation. However, we have to give up one of those prayer meetings to accommodate it, because this is the night that most of the saints are available. Next thing, problems arise in the congregation. No one was looking and Satan crept in unnoticed. 1 Peter 5:8, "Be sober, be vigilant; because your adversary the devil, as a roaring lion, walketh about, seeking whom he may devour:" Let us be alert and be on guard at all times in the spirit. Let us be wise, in discerning the tactics of the enemy. Recognize the weapons of the devil and destroy them before they destroy us. Don't let the enemy seduce any into leading the flock astray.

# 10

Bodies in the Sky

Dream

I entered the area where I live. I looked up in the sky and I saw naked people lying down on their backs. They were male and female, boys and girls of every nation under the sun. I saw a long huge ruler between two of the bodies. A left hand was placed on the ruler and a right hand was beside the ruler. I did not see the body of the person whose hand was on the ruler. As I made a 360-degree turn, I realized that the bodies of people were all beside each other in a circle around the sky in one line. They were all naked. Some were alive and moving their bodies, but they were groaning in pain. Others were lying still as if they were dead. I called out to my daughter as I entered our home, to come outside and take a look up in the sky. We were so stunned to see what we saw. However, I did not understand why they were all in the sky and what had happened to them. We both stood in bewilderment, looking up in the sky at this abnormal scene. I woke up.

In the book of Daniel 5, it is recorded of King Belshazzar who was weighed in the balances and was found lacking. Belshazzar, son of Nebuchadnezzar, knew of the great glory God had given his father and how his father's heart was lifted up in pride. God threw out Nebuchadnezzar from his glorious kingdom. God drove him away from the presence of men, to be like the wild beasts and to live with them, where he ate grass, his body wet with the dew of heaven. Yet, Belshazzar allowed himself to be lifted up against God, by using the holy vessels of God to entertain his entourage, worshipped idols and did not glorify God in whose hand his breath was. In the midst of Belshazzar's celebration there came fingers of a man's hand and wrote against the candlestick on the wall of the palace, and King Belshazzar saw it. The King in the distress of mind, called the astrologers, Chaldeans and the soothsayers, but none could interpret the words written on the wall. At the queen's suggestion, Daniel was called and he gave the interpretation of the words written on the wall. Daniel 5:25-28, "And this is the writing that was written, MENE, MENE, TEKEL, UPAHARSIN. This is the interpretation of the thing: MENE, God hath numbered thy kingdom, and finished it. TEKEL; Thou art weighed in the balances and art found wanting. PERES; Thy kingdom is divided, and given to the Medes and Persians." King Belshazzar reign had come to an end and he was found lacking. He was killed that same night. Darius the Mede, captured the kingdom.

Man has rejected the Living God and has put Him out of his daily activities. Man has become his own god, governing his own self, and applying his own rules. We have forgotten the Sovereign God in whose hand our breath lies. Like King Belshazzar, many have taken the holy things that should be used for the glory of God and has used them for their own pleasure. We are inviting Satan in, when we put God out and dismiss Him from being among us. We have spent time casting out God out of everything, when we should have been casting out devils. God is love and He is the God of justice. The ruler represents the judgement of God. The bodies in the sky were measured against the ruler and none came in full measurement. All were lacking. The left hand on the ruler shows that God is now taking judgement. The right hand beside the ruler indicates that the judgement is not in fullness as if both hands were on the ruler. The right hand represents God's power. God is still merciful and did not give the full consequences, yet. The people lying naked are a result of their shame being exposed. Some will be exposed of their evil deeds so that others will see. Some will die from epidemics and others will experience excruciating suffering and pain. Many will be bereaved of their children. This will be a worldwide occurrence. This is a result of the elevation of sin in the earth. As the population increases so sin increases.

God is being forced out of the lives of people, as this occurs the demonic host will come in and advance their activity in the lives of people who reject the fountain of life. The devil's only agenda for mankind is to steal, kill and destroy. Currently, there are so many chaotic events occurring in the earth, such as fatal uprisings, natural disasters, horrific accidents, innumerable diseases and many more unpleasant endings. The earth has never encountered this magnitude since its creation. All these will increase in frequency, intensity and enormity as we approach the end of the age. St. Matthew 24 and St. Luke 21 both give us a vivid description of the times we are living in.

Church of the living God, be sober and watch. Let us examine ourselves and stay in the love of God. These are the days that are setting the stage for the ushering for the appearance of the Beast, the anti-Christ, the tribulation period, and finally, the reign of the Kingdom of God. The signs of the end of the age are rapidly being fulfilled. The reign of Christ is the ultimate goal. Nevertheless, all these must come to pass before Christ takes His rightful reign. We, who are called by the name of Christ, are not of the night. God has enlightened us. For those who are sleeping, wake up out of your sleep. Many deceptions are around. They are designed to keep us earth bound and not heaven ready. There's a very popular saying among Christians in regards to someone who is extremely heavenly minded. This person who is so heavenly minded is said "to be so heavenly minded, he is no earthly good." Unfortunately, we have become so earthly-minded we are no heavenly good. It is better to be extremely heavenly minded. That is the place of our destination. St. Luke 12:34, "For where your treasure is, there will your heart be also." Our hearts will be focused on the earth, if our treasures are on the earth. Our hearts will be focused on heaven, if our treasures are in heaven. Do not give your crown to anyone. Let us hold on to the Word of God. Recognize the lies of the devil and do not take in any of them. If we don't know God's Word we won't be able to recognize the lies of the devil. We cannot enter into the Kingdom of God, if we do not live a holy life.

Seeing that we are approaching the imminent tribulation period, understand that hard times will come. Demonic activities will increase and are presently increasing rapidly. Satan is a nervous wreck right now, because his time of ultimate punishment is swiftly approaching. His destiny is already fixed and cannot be changed. Every day he is one day closer to being extinct in the Lake of Fire. He is scared, fearful and trembling even as you are reading these words, because he is closer today to his banishment than he was yesterday. He who deceived the whole world will be locked up in a bottomless pit for one thousand years and then cast into the Lake of Fire forever. The book of Revelation told us that Satan lost the battle. Hallelujah, Glory to God in the Highest! Satan will be chained in the bottomless pit. He will not be able to operate. Do we think that Satan is joyously anticipating this coming time in his life? He is pulling out everything that he can to deceive and to have us accompany him in the Lake of Fire. He will do whatever it takes to deceive as many people as he can so that they don't ever enter heaven where he once had the privilege of living and enjoying. He has heightened his mission to steal, kill and destroy. Sadly, a majority of people will fall into his traps and be condemned with him forever. You have the opportunity to change your destiny right now, Satan does not.

Saints, be watchful. Be alert. Be faithful. Do not allow anyone to take your crown. We each have one soul so possess it in righteousness. Let us not let the day of the coming of our Lord and Saviour Jesus Christ, take us unprepared and unaware. Remember our first love, the love of Jesus Christ. Get back to Jesus Christ, our first love. Remember we started the journey to obtain everlasting life. Let us all complete it in victory. This is the understanding of the dream that was revealed to me as I sought for the understanding.

11

Demons among the Children

Dream

I went into a house I previously lived in and as I entered the living room, I encountered a man walking towards me. I asked him what he was doing in here. He didn't answer. At this time, I knew that he was a demon. He kept walking towards me. I ran outside to get my parents. They came to the living room and he had disappeared. As soon as they left, the man reappeared. I called my parents and he suddenly vanished again. My parents left the room and I knew where the man had disappeared to. I decided to go around the corner to another room. I picked up a stick and attacked the man. I pushed the stick in his navel, lifted him up on the stick and took him outside. I started spinning him in the air in the name of Jesus Christ, while he was elevated on the stick. I noticed that as I spun him, there came thousands of other men flying out of him. They were all spinning in a circle in the air. I realized that I was dealing with legions. The atmosphere was so mystical. The demon positioned on the stick kept begging for me to put him down. I brought the stick down and started commanding every one of them, one by one, to go back to their world in the name of Jesus Christ. As I commanded them, they each disappeared into the darkness. I turned and saw a little girl with a doll, sitting and playing among the children on the playground. I knew she was one of the demons in disguise. I went over to her and commanded her in the name of Jesus Christ to leave and go back to her world. She ignored me completely. She was a very stubborn one. I had to speak to her about seven times in the name of Jesus Christ before she moved. She suddenly disappeared into complete darkness. I went back to the man that I had initially placed on the stick. He was crying tears and begging me not to send him back to his world. He told me that he would adjust to my world if I allowed him to stay. I told him "no, you must go back to your world. This is my world, not yours." I commanded him to go back to his world in the name of Jesus Christ, and he vanished into vast darkness.

Waking up was so mystical. I felt like I was not on the earth realm. I was somewhere in a totally different sphere. For the whole day I was walking on the earth but not in the earth. I cannot fully explain the spiritual aspect of it. The Lord had given the interpretation in the dream. This dream reminded me of the incident that occurred with Jesus and the legion of devils that took up residence in the man that had his home among the tombs. In our days, this would be in the cemetery. The recorded incident in St. Luke 8:22-39 tells us that Jesus and the disciples went on a boat across the lake where a great storm met them. The disciples were terrified because the boat was taking in water and Jesus was sleeping. They woke Him up and He reprimanded the wind and the boisterous water and they both became calm. They came to the country of the Gadarenes, where a demon-possessed man met them. In the course of casting out the demonic spirit, Jesus asked the demon in the man that spoke, "What is your name?" The demon replied "My name is Legion: for we are many." (St. Mark 5:9). The demon beseeched Jesus Christ not to send them out of the country but to send them into the swine that were feeding on the mountain. Jesus granted them permission to enter the swine. Of course, the swine ran violently down the mountain and drowned in the sea.

In the dream there were thousands of men flying out of the man. I realized that this was Legion. The one among the children in disguise was very stubborn. The enemy starts his work of stealing, killing and destruction right among the children. The main demon begged me with tears running down his cheeks not to send him back to his world. In trying to deceive me, he said he would adjust to my world if I let him stay. Thank God for the Holy Ghost who discerns. In the name of Jesus Christ the demon was commanded to go back to his world. We have power in the name of Jesus Christ to cast them out. Amen.

Dream #2

I was passing by a playground where some toddlers were playing. I noticed among them were two separate pairs of transparent toddler-size shoes. They were like shiny glass. These two sets of shoes did not have a body in them. There were no feet in them. Yet these two pairs of shoes were running around in the playground and playing with the children. I was the only one who saw them. They were not visible to the eyes of the teachers on the playground. I started speaking in tongues and went on the playground. I began to rebuke unclean spirits in the name of Jesus Christ, who were masquerading around on the playground with the children. I woke up speaking in tongues.

Waking up, I gained understanding of the dream. Unfortunately, there are unclean spirits among the children. The natural eyes cannot see them. These unclean spirits were among the toddlers. The activities of the demonic host started working in them as babies. They don't wait until they are teenagers. They start their work from infancy. We must be proactive and start the training of our children from infancy. Teach them about the Almighty God. Pray and cover them in the blood of

Jesus Christ. Trying to fix them in their teens might be a bit late. Satan and his demons are on assignment to destroy the children from their early years of innocence. The demons will have already done tremendous damage by the time they are teenagers. The seeds are being sown in infancy. By the time they are teenagers, it has become a full-grown tree, producing unacceptable fruits. Act now and train them quickly and often. Please do not allow video games, electronic games, internet games, the movies and television to foster their knowledge. These are strategies designed to destroy them. They become what they behold. For instance, you will see little children running after each other with pretend weapons on the playground. This moves from pretend play to practice on their electronic games, with their final destination on the street with a gun.

Give the little children the opportunity to behold Jesus Christ. Let them behold the good principles you want them to have. They cannot have good values unless we, the adults in their lives, introduce them to it. Children were not created to govern themselves. Love and care enough about their soul to be an active participant in their upbringing. The training in their early years will help them to become what they should become. Use this time wisely.

Dear parents: do not let your children set the rules and standards for their lives. Do not let the children govern and rule you. God allowed you to be your children's parents and not them your parents. If God wanted them to be your parents you would have been born to them. You have in you what they need to govern their lives. Do not let them down. Let me greatly stress this point: Demons are unleashed among the children to take control of their mind and behaviour from infancy, so that the devil can easily control and use them to his advantage, leading to the children's destruction.

Many children will not live past their teens, as we become a more tolerant, acceptable, morally declined society. This is on Satan's agenda. He will wrap himself around them like the snake that he is, strangle them and gobble them up whole like a snake digesting a pig. Let me stress this clearly, Satan does not love anyone. Satan is incapable of loving. His only objective is to steal, kill and destroy every human that he can. His time of final punishment is very close, so he is doing all he can with his demons to take as many people as is possible to the Lake of Fire with him. Our precious little children are not too young for him to use and destroy. Check the news report in every nation and see the end results of the devil's work in the lives of many young people. Many children have become callous in their heart, without any affection for anything or anyone, disrespectful and disobedient to parents and authority.

One morning, I stood by my window praying for the children in the schools, due to the increase of slain young lives in the schools. I asked God to protect the children in the schools, and I heard as plain as ever in a sad and pitiful voice, "I can't, they put me out." I stood at my window, stunned by what I heard. I could not pray another word. I became weak and had to sit on my bed to regain my strength. I kept pondering, "God, You can't? But God, You can do all things." For the whole day I was in a daze. I went to a school program that day. This was in the Christmas season. One of the assistants asked the supervisors if she could show the children a documentary. The supervisor asked her what was the documentary about. The assistant teacher told her that it was about the birth of Jesus Christ. The supervisor said a big "NO, no religious DVD, if it is about Santa Claus then you can show it. They don't want us to show anything with Jesus Christ." Then I heard in the spirit "I can't, they put me out." I barely functioned that afternoon, because I knew that this was real and that I had heard the sad heart of God. I thought to myself, they say December 25th is Jesus Christ's birthday, yet He is not invited or welcomed to come to his birthday party. Everyone else and everything else can come and have a good time, but "Jesus Christ you can stay outside and keep a watch and protect us." In actuality what we are saying is we want Jesus Christ to protect our children but we don't want him in our schools. I encourage every saint to pray for your children every day before sending them to school. Send them to school with Jesus Christ.

In an effort to accommodate everyone, countries that were built on the foundations of Jesus Christ, have disregarded Jesus and welcomed other strange gods that they or Jesus Christ knew not of. In light of this decision, many are paying a price for putting Christ out. Jesus Christ no longer covers them. When you purchase car insurance, the car is covered as long as you keep the policy active. Should the policy lapse or cancel for any reason, the car is no longer covered. The insurance company is no longer liable for any costs incurred by the owner of the vehicle. Should you get into an accident, you will be charged for not having insurance on your vehicle and you will have to find the money to cover the cost of the damage incurred. You will be on your own. We are on our own against Satan, when we walk away from the covering of Jesus Christ. On our own against Satan, without Jesus Christ, we are done for. Human beings are no match for Satan on our own. He is a spirit and is more powerful than humans. Humans cannot outwit Satan. He cannot be detected with the natural eye.

He's been around before man was created. Let's not fool ourselves, we need Jesus Christ. Jesus Christ has overcome the devil.

Dream #3

I was with some children from a school at a camp that appears to be on a farm. There were many other schools and school buses there. The announcement came, that bus #32 was ready to board, which was the bus that I came on. On our way to the bus, I saw a bear cub run into the camp. I told the group of children and teachers that I was with, to run quickly to the bus. They wanted to pet the bear cub but I insisted that they run because if you saw a bear cub chances are the mother was close behind and probably the father too. Then I saw a huge black bear standing upright on its legs at the entrance of the camp. At this everyone started running. The children and teachers that I was with got lost in the frantic commotion. I ran on a bus for safety. This was not the bus I came on. I told the bus driver that there are bears on the premises and this was not my bus. I did not recognize anyone on the bus. I was just going to wait on the bus until this attack was over. I kept praying to God to cover my daughter who was on the trip also, and hoped that she made it on to one of the buses. It now appeared that there were three bears on the premises. These bears were attacking the children. The bus I was on drove off and was exiting the campsite. I told the driver that this is not my bus and I wanted to go on my bus. The bus driver turned the bus back into the compound. He drove around to find my bus but I did not recognize anyone on any of the buses. Teachers and children were standing still in a straight line outside. There was no movement among them because the father bear was standing among the trees behind them. One movement and they would be killed. The driver drove around to the back of the compound to ask one of the camp workers to help me find a ride home. I came off the bus and went into a building where I saw a gentleman I knew. I knew I would make it home safe because the gentleman would give me a ride. I overheard one camp worker telling a teacher that, "Bears would come in the distance outside of the camp site way over the hills but we never thought that they would enter the camp." I came out of the building and stood in front of the door. I saw, a few feet in front of me, an animal that resembled a lama. It stood at the back fence of the campsite. I watched as it lifted up its wing with the feathers of a peacock. Its mouth changed and it took the shape of a dragon. I then realized that it was a dragon and not a lama or a peacock. Black, smelly, gasoline fumes came pouring from its mouth. I ran around the side of the building and hid in a little spot that was in the wall of the building. The Dragon ran with great speed of fury into the campsite where all the children and teachers were and released the fumes from its mouth through the entire compound covering everyone with its fumes. The dragon did not fly, it ran. The scene was one of chaos, panic, confusion and fear. I ran around the other side of the building into a clear path that was set in front of me as the dragon past by me. At this I woke up.

This was one of the most horrible dreams I have ever gotten. The scenery was terrible. It was a terrifying environment full of panic, fear, chaos, confusion, displacement, uncertainties, disbelief, and horror. The fumes the Dragon released were everywhere, over everyone. It was gasoline fumes that were going to choke and kill. The devil is a dragon who, comes to steal, kill and destroy. The three bears are three destructive spirits that had entered the camp to destroy and cause panic. Children are accustomed to stories of bears and dragons. In the vision they are demonic spirits that are on a mission in schools to destroy the lives of children. They are sent into the schools to cause disorder, panic, and terror, to choke, steal, kill, and utterly destroy. The dragon released fumes from his own being; sending it out, covering the environment. The school environment will be saturated with demonic presence. It will be controlled by devils. Many children will be under the influence of demonic control that will present itself as a behaviour. In actuality, it is a demonic spirit operating through the child. It cannot be treated with medicine and counselling. It can only be treated with the saints praying and fasting destroying the works of the devil. There will be an escalation of evil activities and destruction in the schools for Satan has targeted the schools to execute his evil plan.

There weren't any Armed Forces, Security Guards or Park Rangers on the campsite. No one was available to help the teachers and children from the attack that came their way. There was nothing in place to remove the fumes the dragon had released on the compound. This was an unexpected occurrence. It was unnatural and unheard of. With the amount of pitch-black fumes that were poured out on the camp, it would have been impossible for anyone to see and survive. With all the panicking, choking, and gasoline poisoning that were happening, those three bears were able to totally annihilate the children and teachers. The Lord showed me that these are the spirits that have been released into the schools. The campsite was left unguarded because they were not expecting the bears to enter the grounds. The bears were usually a distance away but sadly they entered and were destructive. Never in history have we heard and experienced the catastrophes that are happening in schools today. We have to acknowledge that when we acknowledge God in our ways, He directs our path. Society has said that it is not necessary to have God in the schools among our children. They do not need to learn about God. Sadly, the children are left unguarded and have become open to the devil and his demons.

I was concerned about my daughter hoping she made it on one of the bus safely. The Lord revealed to me that my daughter represents those children. He wanted me to feel it as if it was my own daughter who was caught in the midst of this chaos. My daughter in real life does not work in the school environment. God wants the church to rise up and start praying for our children. These children are innocent. Society has given Satan permission to go in and assault and abuse these children, raping them of their innocence. Children cannot battle the forces of evil by themselves. We need to stand in the gap for them so that they don't get intoxicated with the fumes of the devil. The church is their only defence. They cannot fight the bears and the fumes by themselves. They are vulnerable being exposed to these dangers every school day.

Let us remember that Satan is a dragon, a liar, a thief, a murder, a deceiver, and a slanderer. He is wicked for he is the Wicked One. He is a destroyer. He is evil. Where you find any of these works they are the works of the devil. Many children will be under the influence of the devil doing evil. Many will not know why they do what they do. They will be constrained by the evil one to do it. They feel a strong compelling urge to do the wrong, because they have become the servants of Satan. That strong urge is the devil's strong fumes that he has overcome them with. They will carry out the devil's wish. Let us awake and take charge. Pray continuously. Pray for your children like you have never prayed before. Stand in the gap and win the battle for our children.

12

Sorcery in the Church

Dream

Service had just finished at a church I had attended. I went outside to start my car. The car was making some weird sounds, so I went back inside the church building to get someone to take a look at it. I got someone, and as we were going outside I felt a force very strong pulling at me. It was pulling me backwards up the stairs in the church. I called out for help but everyone ran when they saw that there was no one there pulling me, as I was floating backwards up the stairs. I could not fight it. It was like a vacuum sucking me in. I had no control because I was going backwards. I looked in front of me and I saw a television suspended in the air in front of me. There was a man in it. He appeared to be in a lab with a white overcoat on. The man seemed to be mixing chemicals. I realized that this person was a sorcerer and he was not mixing chemicals. He was mixing potions. The moment I recognized who he was, he took up a bowl of mixture and walked towards me. As

I lifted up my right fist, the television glass broke of its own accord from the power that was in my hand and I hit the man in his face. I hit him with my fist again and he staggered backwards. Then I lifted my hand a third time to hit him; as I lifted my hand, the force that was in my hand was so powerful it jolted me and woke me up just as I was about to hit him again. This all was happening in the church. I woke up exhausted.

Christians involved in sorcery

There are some who are professing Christ and practising sorcery. You have kindled the anger of God. God is angry. Your covetousness has caused you to cast spells in other people's lives. Stop mixing Christianity with witchcraft. Stop walking with special things in your purse, shoes and pocket to ward off and or attract spirits. Stop putting things around your wrist to give you protection. Stop wearing rings on your fingers and chains around your neck that you receive from the sorcerer. Stop wearing special clothes under your clothing to attract you know what. Stop rubbing yourself with the oils the witch gave you to attract and to dispel. Put away all those gadgets that you place around your house, at the entrance of your door, at your windows, in your home, in your car, at your place of employment, in the church and on the church premises. Stop putting things at people's door and around their house in order to bewitch them. Stop burying people's picture and other items in the ground to cause death and other ailments. You, who are involved in these devilish activities, stop casting your evil spells and locking up people in the spirit realm. You are angering God. Put every one of them away. Stop burning candles and incense in your home to ward off evil spirits. Stop using sprays and other items in your home with the intent to clear evil spirits. Stop participating in demonic blood covenants. These are not the teachings and actions of Christ. Stop visiting that "spiritual guide" to get your special bath and engaging in the other rituals that you participate in. 2 Corinthians 6:17, "Wherefore come out from among them, and be ye separate, saith the Lord, and touch not the unclean thing; and I will receive you." Stop talking to the dead to give you directions.

Those who are involved in these conducts are sleeping with the devil, and having fellowship with him. Stop casting spells on people. Stop sprinkling special powder around people's houses. Those of you, who have used witchcraft to destroy people's lives, caused illness to other people's children, caused miscarriages, destroyed marriages, caused businesses to fail, and even caused death, repent and turn from your wicked ways. Stop tampering with people's future. God is going to visit you with a visitation. Quickly repent, for you are going to reap the wickedness you have sown. After you have planted, comes the time of reaping. All the iniquities you have been involved in are coming back to you with interest. Your harvest is coming. Repent, repent, repent and turn from your wicked ways. "Regard not them that have familiar spirits, neither seek after wizards, to be defiled by them: I am the LORD your God." (Leviticus 19:31)

Pastor with his briefcase (Vision)

This happened in reality and not a dream. I was in my room praying alone. I was in a standing position. While I was praying, I saw a pastor with a briefcase in his hand rushing quickly and unnoticeably to go into a store, which appeared to be a palm reading shop. I called out the person's name and turned my eyes to read the store sign, when a force pushed me against the wall in my bedroom. I realized that I had seen something that the enemy did not want me to see. I was literally pushed against the wall.

Leaders, who are using witchcraft to control and manipulate the congregation, stop it. Witchcraft practitioners, whether you do your craft at the graveyard, go to a sorcerer, the Obeah man, the Witch doctor, the Voodoo priest under a tree, use of black magic, chant to the moon and stars, or have spirit forum, repent. God is about to expose you. Don't be deceived; God will bring all these evil works into judgement. God is watching and He is very angry. He saw each time you crept into that place unnoticed by others, paid your fee and made your request to destroy others. Stop sending evil spirits to people's home. Cleanse yourself of these filthy actions.

For those who meddled with these mediums to get wealth, position and the likes, your sin will be uncovered. Repent. This is committing whoredom with unclean spirits and adding iniquity to iniquity. Being involved in this whoredom has caused you to defile yourself. You have embraced the spirit of Jezebel with her whoredom and witchcraft. Read 2 Kings 9:22. When we choose to do these things to others we are in actuality telling the Lord this is how we want to be treated. Let me remind us of Galatians 6:7 NASB, "Do not be deceived; God is not mocked: for whatever a man sows, this he will also reap". Reaping time is coming. Repent. I encourage everyone to let us send out only what we desire to receive for ourselves. For surely, good or bad, it will be returned to us. St. Luke 6:38, "Give and it shall be given unto you, good measure pressed down, and shaken together, and running over, shall men give into your bosom. For with the same measure that ye mete withal it shall be measured to you again." You shall receive what you sent out pressed down, shaken together and running over. It will be multiplied and run over with interest and with God's justly divine portion return to you.

Use the Word of God

Follow the scriptures. Many gadgets have innocently come into the church, such as holy water, soap, salt, consecrated cloth etc. Many of these devices are used to enhance our faith. It is very easy for these things to become doctrine. Careful what you use and give yourself to. The only washing we need is in the blood of the Lamb. If the blood of the Lamb cannot wash it away, it cannot be washed away. Be not deceived. Romans 1:17, "For therein is the righteousness of God revealed from faith to faith: as it is written, The just shall live by faith."

The Bible tells us in James 5:13-15 "Is any among you afflicted? Let him pray. Is any merry? Let him sing psalms. Is any sick among you? Let him call for the elders of the church; and let them pray over him, anointing him with oil in the name of the Lord: and the prayer of faith shall save the sick, and the Lord shall raise him up; and if he have committed sins, they shall be forgiven him." Children of God, stick to the Word. Don't bring in anything that the Word did not endorse to make it into a doctrine and cause saints to rely on these material things to stimulate their faith. When we decide to make changes to God's Words, this will lead to severe consequences.

Let us be careful that our faith is not found relying on these things. Satan is an imposter and a false manifestation of truth. He will use it as a doctrine in the church. Soon we begin to rely on these things as instruments of healing instead of in the Holy Ghost. Next we are found buying these things to bring healing and deliverance to ourselves. Be very wise. Be cautious. Satan is cunning. The Bible tells us of "laying on of hands" in St. Mark 16:15-18 and "anointing with oil" in James 5:14-16, it is the "prayer of faith" that shall save the sick. In Acts 19:11-12, God performed mighty miracles by Paul's hands and the people brought handkerchiefs and aprons to touch Paul's body and carried them to the sick and diseased. They were all healed and the evil spirits went out of those who were demon possessed. Stay on the Word and pray the Word. I Corinthians 10:21-22, "Ye cannot drink the cup of the Lord, and the cup of devils: ye cannot be partakers of the Lord's table, and of the table of devils. Do we provoke the Lord to jealousy? Are we stronger than he?" Why have many gone to fellowship with darkness? Why are we provoking God? Why are we communing with devils? We are called to be holy. We cannot hold to God and hold to the devil. We cannot walk the path of God and the path of the devil at the same time. We can only hold so much in our hands; eventually we have to let something go. Even though we have two feet, we cannot walk two paths at the same time. We can only go one way. How is it that some are walking with God and walking with the devil?

Let us carry the word of God in our hearts and speak it with our mouth because that is what we need. As long as our sins have been washed away in the blood of Jesus Christ, we are filled with the Holy Ghost and the Word of God is abiding in us and we are abiding in Christ, we don't need any device to travel or live with in regards to spiritual living. We don't need to burn any candle or incense in our home to chase out any devil. God has given us power over all the powers of the enemy. Use the Word of God and chase him out, if he enters your home. Let us evict those devils out of our lives and cast them back into the world of darkness where they originated. It is written in St. Luke 9:1, "Then he called his twelve disciples together, and gave them power and authority over all devils, and to cure diseases." St. Luke 10:19 says, "Behold, I give unto you power to tread on serpents and scorpions, and over all the power of the enemy: and nothing shall by any means hurt you."

Let us use fasting and prayer in the Holy Ghost, so that there will be a demonstration of the Holy Ghost. The Word of God is committed to us and Jesus Christ Himself has committed Himself to us. Let us use His Words. He backs up His Words and He will always honour His Word. His Words were spoken years ago and the Word spoken is a spirit and eternal. God's Word cannot die, be depleted or worn out. God's Word is present. Again, I plead with the saints, who are involved in these practices, stop carrying things in your purse and pocket. These unholy practices contradict the teaching of the Word of God. Let us carry the Word of God in our heart. Be set free from this bondage that you have roped yourself into, in the name of Jesus Christ.

13

Praying Demonic Prayers

Dream

One Sunday afternoon after morning service at the assembly where we worship, my family went to have a nap before going back to the night service. I heard a knock on my bedroom door and someone sobbing, while I was asleep. I told the person to come in. My daughter came in crying. I tried to find out why she was crying so much, because she is not a crier. She kept saying, "they are blocking me." I sat on the bed and she came and dropped down on her knees, placed her head in my lap and kept saying, "they are blocking me." I realized that she had a dream and she was not fully out of it. I laid my hands on her and prayed until she was settled. Then she proceeded to tell me the dream, which is relevant to the subject being exposed.

The dream

She went with a friend to a church service. As they entered one of the doors to the building, a lady dressed in a full red and black dress, red shoes, red gloves, red head coverings, red lipstick and red eye shadow, met them at the door. The lady told them that they couldn't enter through that door. They went to another door to get in the building and there was another lady dressed in the same outfit. The lady told them that they couldn't enter there either. They proceeded to a third entrance where there was another lady standing in the door, dressed in the same manner, blocking them from entering. Her friend managed to push her way into the building, but two others fully dressed in red and black outfit, a man and a woman, held her by her arms and led her away from the door. They told her to come with them. She was fighting not to go but they held her and took her to another entrance where they went into a small room in the church. When she entered the room, there were many of them dressed in the same red and black outfits. They were all praying and telling God to do terrible things to people. A set was praying for a certain man to die in his sleep. They told her to come and join them. She told them "no, I will not join you, this is not right." She woke up crying, "they are blocking me."

Those who are assembling together, to pray wicked prayers, stop it. Stop praying wicked prayers over people's lives, because you don't like them or because they did something to you that made you angry. Stop praying for people to die in their sleep. Stop praying satanic, hateful prayers to God. God will not hear you. Stop the wickedness. It is devilish and an evil disease.

Unforgiveness in the church

One of the reasons for unanswered prayers is unforgiveness. The spirit of unforgiveness has filled the heart of many pastors and saints alike. Many saints are finding it very hard to let go of grudges and to forgive. The person, who is holding on to unforgiveness, is only keeping his or her own self-bound. When we don't forgive others, we are hindering God from forgiving us. In St. Matthew 6:14-15 it tells us, "For if ye forgive men their trespasses, your heavenly Father will also forgive you: But if ye forgive not men their trespasses, neither will your Father forgive your trespasses." What we are actually saying to God is to treat me like I treat the one who wronged me. The church is full with a lot of unforgiven people. Jesus gave us permission to forgive others, even when we go to Him in prayer. St. Mark 11:25 NASB says, "Whenever you stand praying, forgive, if you have anything against anyone, so that your Father who is in heaven will also forgive you your transgressions". We all need to be forgiven. Let us forgive each other. It is okay to forgive others.

Forgiveness is available for all. We all have it in us to forgive others. Forgiveness is possible.

There are many unforgiven pastors preaching, unforgiven prophets prophesying, unforgiven teachers teaching, unforgiven altar workers praying for people and such like them. There are some saints who choose to let some saints' sins go and hold some saints' sins hostage by refusing to forgive them. We need to put that kind of attitude away and stop holding people's sins for ransom. There is only one spotless Lamb of God, who takes away the sins of the world. Ephesians 4:31-32, "Let all bitterness, and wrath, and anger, and clamour, and evil speaking, be put away from you, with all malice: And be ye kind one to another, tender-hearted, forgiving one another, even as God for Christ's sake hath forgiven you." See also Colossians 3:13. Beloved, unforgiveness is not worth losing our relationship with the Lord Jesus Christ. In St. Matthew 5:39-49, Jesus Christ told us how to deal with evil, our enemies, those who curse us, those who hate us, and with those who despitefully use us and persecute us. Nowhere did he tell us to pray evil on them. The Word of God states in Romans 12:21, "Be not overcome of evil, but overcome evil with good." We are being overcome by the evil others have done us, when we take the route to pray for evil things to happen to them. In this case the evil is dominating us and causing us to accomplish its desire. In the end this will only destroy us. This is the desire of our adversary, Satan. Leave vengeance to God, it belongs to Him and He will repay it. See Romans 12:19-20. Our part is to heap up coals of fire on our enemies' head, by doing good to them, not to take revenge. This act of praying evil is not of God. If any of us has participated in this, let us repent and turn away from these kinds of prayers.

Let's adopt the spirit of Stephen who was stoned for the word of the testimony of Jesus Christ. Acts 7:60 states, "And he kneeled down, and cried with a loud voice, Lord, lay not this sin to their charge. And when he had said this, he fell asleep." Stephen released the sin that they committed against him to God. When we release the evil that others have done to us to God through forgiveness, it's like giving up the ghost of it, so that it has no authority over us. Holding on to the grudge will only give place for its ghost to haunt us. The act that was done to us is past. It is just the ghost of it remains. We need to release that ghost through forgiveness. Let it rest in peace.

Let's consider Jesus Christ who is our example of all righteous acts. On the cross at His crucifixion He cried "Father, forgive them for they know not what they do." He had the power and authority to call angels to destroy those who were killing Him. Yet, He refrained from doing so. We are to pray the same prayer of forgiveness as Jesus Christ prayed for people. If we are engaged in praying any other prayer than the prayer of forgiveness for those who offends us, it will only lead to ineffective, powerless and defeated lives. This causes us to live under a brass heaven because we are not being forgiven by God.

Peter, at one time in the scriptures, took a sword and cut off a man's ear with the intention to defend and protect Jesus. Jesus put the man's ear back on and healed it. He told Peter to put up his sword. St. Luke 22:50-51, "And one of them smote the servant of the high priest, and cut off his right ear. And Jesus answered and said, Suffer ye thus far. And he touched his ear, and healed him." The same incident recorded in St. John 18:10-11 states, "Then Simon Peter having a sword drew it, and smote the high priest's servant, and cut off his right ear. The servant's name was Malchus. Then said Jesus unto Peter, Put up thy sword into the sheath: the cup which my Father hath given me, shall I not drink it?" These men came to arrest Jesus and were going to have Him killed, yet Jesus healed Malchus' ear. Coming in disagreement with this action would mean conforming to the method of Satan. These are the days when Christians are partaking in taking up and exercising the physical sword. Unforgiveness is a weapon of Satan and seem to be the weapon of choice for many who are called to be saints. We are not here to destroy men's life.

We are here to tear down and destroy the works of the devil that are being performed through men.

On another occasion, James and John asked Jesus if they should command fire to come down from heaven to consume the Samaritans, because they did not respond to Jesus' message as the disciples expected. Jesus turned and rebuked them, telling them "you do not know of what spirit you are of." Jesus said He did not come to destroy men's lives. See St. Luke 9:54-56. Many of our attitudes are like Peter, James and John, ready to draw the wrong sword and to call down destructive fire to consume one another through prayer. Notice that it was the three closest ones to Jesus who were ready to destroy lives. Jesus Christ corrected these disciples who had the wrong understanding of the scripture. Let us not use the scriptures wrongfully to justify our personal vendettas. Now beloved saints, we are washed and are clean, let us live like 1 Peter 4:12-13, "Beloved, think it not strange concerning the fiery trial which is come to try you, as though some strange thing happened unto you: But rejoice, inasmuch as ye are partakers of Christ's sufferings; that, when his glory shall be revealed, ye may be glad also with exceeding joy."

Consider this; if you go through this life never offended by anyone, never spoken evil of or you never offend or speak evil of anyone, then you were never born. This is why we need to operate at all times in the Fruit of the Spirit, Galatians 5:22-23, "But the fruit of the Spirit is love, joy, peace, longsuffering, gentleness, goodness, faith, meekness, temperance: against such there is no law." This is to be done to all human beings, as recorded in St. Matthew 5:45, "That ye may be the children of your Father which is in heaven: for he maketh his sun to rise on the evil and on the good, and sendeth rain on the just and on the unjust." The apostle Paul told us that witchcraft and the likes are all works of the flesh. Galatians 5:19-21, "Now the works of the flesh are manifest, which are these: Adultery, fornication, uncleanness, lasciviousness, idolatry, witchcraft, hatred, variance, emulations, wrath, strife, seditions, heresies, envying, murders, drunkenness, revelling, and such like: of the which I tell you before as I have also told you in time past, that they which do such things shall not inherit the kingdom of God." This admonition of Paul was written to born again Christians. Let us not allow resentment, bitterness, unforgiveness, hatred and such like sins, cause us to be separated from God. See Isaiah 59. We are called to operate at a higher standard of living because of the Holy Ghost. We are not of the darkness, we are of the light.

Pray God's word

Line up all prayers with the Word of God. Pray the Word of God back to Him. St. John 1:1, "In the beginning was the Word, and the Word was with God, and the Word was God." God is His Word. God honours His Word. God's Word is His will. When we use God's words, it is as if God is the one speaking His word, and His Words will not return unto Him void. He has given us His Words in James 4:7, "Submit yourselves therefore to God. Resist the devil, and he will flee from you." The only way to get the devil to take flight is to administer the Word of God. Early morning prayers work wonders to your day. They are powerful and it does put your day in order. You give God the first part of the day, and He'll give you the rest of the day. I encourage those who are using gadgets and things that has no business in the things of God, be conformed to the Word of God. Let the Word of God work for you and not witchcraft or Satanic mechanics. Put away these evil far from you and return to God. Follow the Lord Jesus Christ and stop following devils. Cleanse yourself from all uncleanness and follow righteousness.

14

Sold to the Highest Bidders

As I was waking up one morning I heard "Bidding Machine." I said, "God what is a bidding machine?" That didn't make any sense to me.

Times of giving of offerings in many churches, has become a time of "Bidding for Dollars." The collector of the offering says that he or she got a word from the Lord that, for example, there are twenty people with $1000, and God has a special miracle for you. So, twenty people bring their money in, bidding and paying for miracles. They continue bidding for miracles at different prices. The lower the price is the less the financial miracle. Those who don't have the preferred offering, get to have the remnant or the scrapings or nothing at all. The church has become a "Bidding Machine."

It is not God's intention that people be pressured into bringing in what they do not have and can't afford. Sometimes it sound like the church is having an auction for blessings and miracles. I went to a church convention some time ago. The person collecting the offering said he spoke to God in the evening regarding the amount to be collected for the night's offering. He asked ten people to stand with $1000, for God said he is going to open the business for them. It took about fifteen minutes for ten people with $1000 to stand and make that commitment. After the ten stood the person collecting the offering confirmed that these are the ones that God was talking about. They were each put in the pastor's chair to sit. All the pastors present, laid hands on them and they were prayed for. They were told that the anointing of the pastor was upon them and they would receive their financial miracle. I thought about those who want to start a business and those who have a business and would like to see it flourish but do not have $1000 in their name to offer for this great guaranteed blessing.

A few nights later in the week, I felt in my spirit to go back to the service. Only to hear the pastor ramping and raging about those who came up and gave dishonoured cheques of $1000 in the offering. It appeared that about eighty percent of them gave a cheque that was not honoured by the bank because they did not have that amount of money in their account. The pastor said that the blessing that he gave them, he took it back because God gave him the authority to do so. I was in disbelief by what I heard. I thought it was a guaranteed blessing from the Lord that He had confirmed and sanctioned these persons for this "opening business blessings." Again, I had the opportunity at another time to hear a pastor say to the congregation regarding tithes and offerings, because the people were slow in coming with them; "didn't you know that I can curse you, for God gave me power to curse you?" As a matter of fact, I heard this statement out of the mouth of two pastors. At what point does the word of Jesus come into effect that we should bless and not curse others? St. Matthew 6:44-45, "But I say unto you, Love your enemies, bless them that curse you, do good to them that hate you, and pray for them which despitefully use you, and persecute you; That ye may be the children of your Father which is in heaven: for He maketh his sun to rise on the evil and on the good, and sendeth rain on the just and on the unjust."

The apostle Paul continued the word in Romans 12:14, "Bless them which persecute you: bless, and curse not." There is no place that said you ought to curse the saints, God's people. Even for those who persecute us, God did not give us permission to curse. How are we so bold to curse God's people? St. James 3:10 states, "Out of the same mouth proceedeth blessing and cursing. My brethren, these things ought not so to be." God said feed my sheep and lambs to Peter in St John 21:15:17,

He didn't say curse and kill them. We need to realize that when we curse people we are not abiding in the Word of God. Let us not give ourselves to practice this manipulative spirit of cursing people to fulfill our own egotistical desires. Leave the cursing and revenge to God. He knows how to administer to everyone what is needful and necessary. We judge by our eyesight but God weighs the thoughts, actions and heart. Let God take care of the contents of the heart. He will do justly.

God has designed for the saints to bring in all the tithes and offering into the storehouse, the church. See Malachi 3:6-12. This is a direct command of God, to be honoured always. The time of giving of tithes and offering to God is a very sacred part of our worship to the Lord. This time is not to be treated lightly. Something from our hand is being given to God directly. This is a physical thing but has great spiritual implications. Many of us are found guilty of not honouring God's command in tithes and offerings. This is a direct violation of the Word of God. To not participate in this command is the sin of disobedience. The tithes and offerings are holy unto God. Once it is given to the Lord Jesus Christ, it becomes sacred. It is not unclean. Whatever we give to the Lord has become holy, as long as it is given in the prescribed requirement of God. In Malachi 3:10, "Bring ye all the tithes into the storehouse, that there may be meat in mine house, and prove me now herewith, saith the Lord of hosts, if I will not open you the windows of heaven, and pour you out a blessing, that there shall not be room enough to receive it."

I have seen in a worship service, the saints brought their monetary offerings to God and laid it on the altar. The offering was blessed and I saw a pastor walk all over the money that was offered to God and is holy unto the Lord. This was to show the congregation that money is nothing. However, when it is given to the Almighty God, it becomes holy. Be careful and wise in our action. Don't allow our fleshy zeal to cause us to sin against God. Let us repent and turn to God in our giving of tithes and offerings.

Another deception that has crept in the church is paying for healing. Break away from this deception. Those who are encouraging people to give money for their healing, deliverance, miracles and so on, you need to search the scriptures and find where in the Word of God that such an act was commissioned. In Acts 8:20-23, Simeon the sorcerer came to Peter and John to purchase power that whosoever he laid hands on; they would receive the Holy Ghost. Peter's response was a swift and firm rebuke. Those who participate in monetary contributions for blessings, check where you are standing. Are you in the gall of bitterness and in the bondage of iniquity? The gifts of God cannot be purchased with money. It is all purchased with the blood of Jesus Christ. Let us be careful and wise in our administration of the Word and presentation of Jesus Christ. Jesus commissioned the disciples and sent them out in St. Matthew 10:8 saying, "Heal the sick, cleanse the lepers, raise the dead, cast out devils: freely ye have received, freely give." They were not commissioned to do this at a cost. Many have become covetous because they were eager for money and have turned from the truth to teaching lies and will eventually pierce themselves with many sorrows. We can see this in display in many lives today.

15

The Face in the Sky Preaching the Gospel

Dream

I attended an outdoor church service. I was standing on a porch with some people, while some were standing on the grass. It was like a sea of church people. I looked in the sky and I saw a face in the sky like the shape of a huge moon. It did not have a body. Then, I saw a man in white clothing standing on top of a mountain. The man was communicating with the face in the sky. Anything that the face told the man to say, he repeated it to the people, but the people were not listening or responding. The face came out of the sky and came down to talk to the people himself. He was telling the people what to do and to repent, as he went through the crowd. He gave someone standing beside me a paper bag with things in it, as he came by me. Suddenly, I heard someone shouted with a loud voice "there's $1.5 million hidden in a certain person's bathroom, behind the toilet bowl." The whole *crowd of church folks took off running with speed to find the money. I noticed that everyone went running, so I took off running too, following the crowd to see who gets the money. People were tumbling over each other trying to get the money. Some were writing cheques to get this money. Everyone was so determined to get this money that no one cared to hear the message and to find out what was in the brown paper bag that the face gave to the person. The receptionist said to me, when I asked her, that no one got the money because it belonged to the person who owned the bathroom.*

I was disturbed by the dream when I woke up. It bothered me that we did not listen and respond to the message or see what was in the bag that was given to the person. I sought the Lord for the understanding of the dream.

We are living in a time where people are refusing to listen to the true Ministers of God. These men and women of God, seek the face of God continually, and operate in the Holy Ghost. God has given them the "Word of Life" and gifts for our lives. We have turned away from hearing them and are running after "tellers" telling us where to find money. God has special gifts for the church but we are too busy chasing what is not even ours, that we don't have time to hear Him and to accept His gifts. In the dream, the money was behind the toilet bowl, the filthiest place. Yet no one cared where the money was located and that it wasn't his or hers. It didn't even matter that it was located where waste matters that are excreted from the body were disposed of. People were willing to write cheques to pay for the money. They preferred to chase after money than to listen to sound doctrine. We have turned away from the message of The Cross to pursue the message of prosperity. Let us remember that God is the owner of the earth. He has entrusted the earth to us to take care of it. We will leave everything that we were entrusted with. We will not take any of the riches with us.

The message of prosperity in regards to material things has infiltrated the church to the point that the mass come to church to hear a positive word of how God is going to bless their barns, full and running over. Every "teller" that comes to town has a word of monetary prosperity. We go to have him or her lay hands on us and to speak a word to us that is positive. Some even dare to give dates that things were going happen for us. We get excited and say, "O, this one is a man of God." We waited, the time came and passed, the next year came, and there is no sign of the word spoken. This message of gaining money is sickening the Lord Jesus Christ. Preach Jesus Christ. Jesus did not teach a prosperity message of money to the disciples. Neither did Jesus commission them to preach and teach it. The gospels and the epistles do not proclaim it. The Bible does not bear record of such preaching. St. Matthew 19:19-20, "Go ye therefore, and teach all nations, baptizing them in the name of the Father, and of the Son, and of the Holy Ghost: Teaching them to observe all things whatsoever I have commanded you: and, lo, I am with you always, even unto the end of the world." This is the commission. The gospel message has not changed.

The first followers of Jesus Christ, those who He taught His Words to and commanded to teach His Words to all nations went out and did exactly as He said. Acts 2:36-42, "Therefore, let all Israel know assuredly, that God hath made that same Jesus, whom ye have crucified, both Lord and Christ. Now when they heard this, they were pricked in their heart, and said unto Peter and to the rest of the apostles, men and brethren, what shall we do? Then Peter said unto them, Repent, and be baptized every one of you in the name of Jesus Christ for the remission of sins, and ye shall receive the gift of the Holy Ghost. For the promise is unto you, and to your children, and to all that are afar off, even as many as the Lord our God shall call. And with many other words did he testify and exhort, saying, save yourselves from this untoward generation. Then they that gladly received his word were baptized: and the same day there were added unto them about three thousand souls." There is nothing in the teachings of Christ to encourage the saints pursuing ill gain. Jesus spoke to Peter and Andrew, in St. Matthew 4:19, "And he saith unto them, Follow me, and I will make you fishers of men." He did not say fishers of wealth.

Jesus said to the rich young ruler, who proclaimed that he kept all the commandments from his youth, to sell all that he has and give to the poor. This young ruler truthfully kept all the commandments but money was an idol in his life. Money is not impure. God is not against money. He is against the place and priority that money occupies in people's life. St. Luke 18:21-23, "And he said, All these have I kept from my youth up. Now when Jesus heard these things, he said unto him, Yet lackest thou one thing, sell all that thou hast, and distribute unto the poor, and thou shall have treasures in heaven: and come follow me." Upon hearing the requirement of Jesus, he went away bitterly and could not follow Jesus because he had much wealth. This young ruler lacked hospitality and compassion towards the poor. The idea of parting with his wealth to give to the poor was unbearable for him. Jesus touched the god who sat in his heart, his wealth. Jesus was not against the riches of the young ruler. He dealt with the conditions of his heart, because his riches took priority over everything. Jesus wants us, His followers, to make Him the Lord of our lives, and not our wealth. This young ruler could not bring himself to have Jesus Christ as Lord of his wealth. Having Jesus Christ as Lord of his wealth meant, distributing it to the poor. He made a decision not to have eternal life by refusing to give up control of his wealth.

Do not misunderstand the message. There are those who will be rich in the church. Many will be exceptional business people. Some will be great investors. Some will have great careers that will gain them great wealth. So do not take the message out of context. We need to have money in the church. We need to be able to support the ministry, missionaries who are preaching the gospel in foreign lands, and the Kingdom in general. There are expenses associated with preaching the gospel. God has made provision for this through His saints. Some saints become rich so that they can distribute to the necessities of the poor and the needs that arise. God has given them the spirit of compassion and hospitality. This is dealing strictly with those whose motive is strictly prosperity in money for selfish reasons. They preach Christ for the purpose of gain, making merchandise of people. Their main preaching is material gain and self-development. Now and again they might remember the Cross. The coming of the Lord Jesus Christ is rarely ever mentioned, and for some, it is nowhere on their agenda. They are more interested in building their kingdoms on the earth and not too concerned about building the heavenly Kingdom. These are they, where money has changed the focus of the Cross. Don't let the accumulation of wealth take pre-eminence over the gospel. Focus on the Cross.

God has given some of us the privilege to reach the world with the gospel. We have the opportunity to speak to millions. What are we preaching to them? Are we preaching the Cross or self-improvement without the blood of Jesus Christ? Are we telling the world that they must be "born again" to enter heaven? Preach to them repentance. Warn them of the times we are living in. Those of us who know the truth, and the signs of Jesus Christ coming, teach it to the people. Romans 10:14, "How shall they hear without a preacher?" That's what preachers are here for. Get as many people save as possible. Leaders, you are responsible for what you teach the people. Angels of the church, the Word of God declares in St. Luke 24:47, "And that repentance and remission of sins should be preached in his name among all nations, beginning at Jerusalem." This is the mandate of the church. It first started at Jerusalem with the Apostles. Now let's take it to the end. Leaders, you know there is only one way to God, and that is through Jesus

Christ. The Book of Acts 4:12 declares: "Neither is there salvation in any other, for there is none other name under heaven given among men, whereby we must be saved." Preach it. Teach it. Live it. St. John 14:6, "Jesus saith unto him, I am the way, the truth, and the life: no man cometh unto the Father, but by me."

Let's not compromise the gospel. Our identity is in Jesus Christ. Many will refuse to accept this call to repentance especially on the subject of money because money has already bound some. We cannot serve God and material wealth. When anything in our life means more to us than God, that thing has become an idol. St Matthew 6:24 told us "No man can serve two masters: for either he will hate the one, and love the other; or else he will hold to the one, and despise the other. Ye cannot serve God and mammon." Mammon means money. Are we longing for God or are we longing for wealth? What are we thirsting for?

16

Welcome to Today's Laodicea Church

Revelation 3:14-22, "And unto the angel of the church of the Laodiceans write; These things saith the Amen, the faithful and true witness, the beginning of the creation of God; I know thy works, that thou art neither cold nor hot: I would thou wert cold or hot. So then because thou art lukewarm, and neither cold or hot, I will spue thee out of my mouth. Because thou sayest, I am rich, and increased with goods, and have need of nothing; and knowest not that thou art wretched, and miserable and poor, and blind, and naked: I counsel thee to buy of me gold tried in the fire, that thou mayest be rich; and white raiment, that thou mayest be clothed, and that the shame of thy nakedness do not appear; and anoint thine eyes with eyesalve, that thou mayest see. As many as I love, I rebuke and chasten: be zealous therefore, and repent. Behold, I stand at the door, and knock: if any man hear my voice, and open the door, I will come in to him and will sup with him, and he with me. To him that overcometh will I grant to sit with me in my throne even as I also overcame, and am set down with my Father in his throne. He that hath an ear, let him hear what the Spirit saith unto the churches.

"I know thy works"

The state of being lukewarm is sickening to the stomach of Jesus Christ. Jesus said, you are lukewarm, so He is going to spit you out of His mouth. An individual doesn't go back and eat vomit when it is excreted from his mouth. To go back and eat vomit is an indication of some serious mental disturbance in the mind. Someone returning his to vomit is sickening. Dogs are known to return to their vomit.

The Laodicea church had absolutely nothing good that Jesus Christ could commend them for. All the other six churches had something that they were applauded for. This is the church age we are living in. These are the times in which the church has mixed the world's system, beliefs and practices with the Kingdom of God, resulting in a temperature that is lukewarm. Church of the living God, we cannot mix that which is holy with that which is unholy; this only generates ungodliness. Have we become friends of the world and the enemies of God?

Have we forgotten what the Word says about friendship with the world? James 4:4, "Ye adulterers and adulteresses, know ye not that the friendship of the world is enmity with God? Whosoever therefore will be a friend of the world is the enemy of God." I must say God has many enemies in the church in this age.

The Church cannot accept and endorse anything that the Word of God is against, even if the world legalized it. The church cannot partake of it. Psalms 119:89, "Forever O Lord, thy word is settled in the heaven." His Words are already established. The Word of God is not up for debate or review. His Words cannot and will not be updated, to allow or give permission to justify any and all modern ungodly conducts. The whole counsel of God has been finalized from before the foundation of the earth. Isaiah 40:8, "The grass withereth, the flower fadeth: but the word of our God shall stand for ever," and St. Matthew 24:35 declares "Heaven and earth shall pass away, but my words shall not pass away."

God will never alter, amend, adjust, change, or modify His commandments, laws or ordinances that He has established, to accommodate any person's, group's, community's or country's affection and lust. God's Word does not submit or conform to anyone; we do the submitting and conforming to His Words. Be not deceived by these seducing spirits. If what is being presented is not in compliance with the Word of God, the saints cannot accept it. It matters not how much agenda we come up with and what is on the agenda, whether hidden or public and how many parliament hearings it goes through. God will never alter His word to fit our agenda. He will never sanction sin. The Church cannot sanction unrighteousness, neither can we redefine righteousness. Should any saint presently be involved in any decision or change that is a direct violation of the Word of God, relinquish your part in it immediately and repent. We must reject every lie of the devil. The Church has no alliance with the world's system that is against the teachings of God's Words. We cannot be involved in changing the divine laws of God. Neither can we adapt, integrate and incorporate any laws, ordinances or commandments of God that any man has changed. We cannot endorse any such changes into the church. Saints of the living God, we can never violate any laws of God and get blessings. God forbid. What God has condemned, the saints cannot go in front or behind God and condone. Let us remember that it is the Word of God that judges our lifestyle, actions and choice. It is before God we will stand and give account of our lifestyle that we have lived here on earth. It is God who will say depart from me, and it is God who will say welcome into the joy of my rest. See St. Matthew 25:31-46. It is not God's will that we dishonour our bodies with each other. Many have already crossed the line in these areas. Neither is it His desire for us to pollute ourselves with devils. Our bodies are God's dwelling place and He needs to dwell in a clean sanctuary...our bodies. 1 Corinthians 6:19, "What? Know ye not that your body is the temple of the Holy Ghost which is in you, which ye have of God, and that ye are not your own?" God will never be mocked. We will always reap what we plant. Galatians 6:7, "Be not deceived; God is not mocked: for whatsoever a man soweth, that shall he also reap." We will all harvest anything that we plant in our bodies. Some are already reaping a tremendous uncontrollable harvest. This is a result of planting.

This letter to the Laodicea church was written to the angel of the church. These are the pastors, bishops, and those who oversee the flock of God. The angel of the church has the mandate, authority, word and mission of Jesus Christ. The saints carry out the instructions of the leaders. Leaders, do what you were put in leadership to do. There is a charge from God on your life to feed the flock the Word of God. Get the flock that you oversee, dressed and ready for the gathering of the saints to Christ. If there was ever a time when many of the angels of the church are full of riches and increased with goods and have need of nothing, is now. Take a look around and you'll see. They stated that all the people God used in the Old Testament were rich. This included Abraham, David, Job, Solomon among others. So God wants us to be rich. The Bible warns us of the deceitfulness of riches. Unfortunately, many have allowed their riches to deceive them. In their riches they are not aware that they are wretched, miserable, poor, blind and naked. This is a very sad state. The Laodicea church is full of material things and in want of nothing, yet poor in spiritual things. Material things do not attract Jesus into our lives; it is the spiritual things that get His attention.

The Laodicea church is an independent church, which prides itself of being a great intellectual church that is full of words, but lacks the demonstration of the power in the Holy Ghost. This church is like a woman who is divorced from her husband but continues to use his name though she has no relationship with him. Laodicea church functions without God. It is emancipated from God and is no longer under His headship. People of God, when we choose to do things, without acknowledging God, we are declaring our independence from Him. Our actions demonstrate that we are sufficient by ourselves. We are, in fact, stating that we can perform and accomplish things on our own.

Jesus Christ came down to examine the works and accomplishments of the Laodicea Church as He did the previous six churches. The Laodicea Church got a big "FF" fat and failed, on their report card. The Laodicea Church was overweight with material things. Absolutely nothing in this church had anything that represented Jesus Christ. There was nothing there to work with. Jesus Christ was not found among the candlesticks (church). By the time the pastors were finished with the church, Christ was not found among the saints. He was found outside the door knocking, hoping that someone would hear His knock and let Him in. They used the name of Jesus to gather their riches but Jesus was not with them. They put Him outside while they focus on getting more goods. Temporally, they were rich and fat in the natural. Spiritually, they were in poverty and naked.

Today's Laodicea church has many shortcomings. This church tolerates evil and those that are evil. Iniquity has found itself in the church and the people have left their first love, Jesus Christ. They endorse those who say they are of Christ and are not, when their doctrine proved that they are churches of Satan. These are all false teaching, designed to trip up the people of God, by teaching them to eat spiritual demonic meals, causing them to commit spiritual whoredom. This is orchestrated by the devil and cleverly integrated into today's church. They have compromised their relationship with God by allowing that old spirit Jezebel, which called herself a prophetess to teach and to seduce God's servants to commit fornication and to eat things offered to idols. So many have risen up in today's church and have given themselves the title of prophets and prophetesses, operating by the spirit of Jezebel, directly under the mandate and power of Satan. These seduce God's people with lies and caused them to eat Satan's filth as meals. These are direct messengers of Satan, carrying out his lust. Today's Laodicea Church has a reputation of being alive but are dead and some are on life support. All that's left is for God to pull the plug. Many of these churches have a reputation of being alive but are full of dead works. They are working but it is futile. They look like they are progressing but gaining grounds for Satan, not for God. Many have risen up and have called themselves Christians and are not. They are of the synagogue of Satan, teaching lies. Repent and turn away from this idolatry.

Jesus Christ still stretched out his hands to the Laodicea church. He said come, buy gold tried in the fire, so you can be rich. Put on white raiment to clothe you that your shame and nakedness will be covered. Come and anoint your eyes with eyesalve so that you may see. As many as He loves, He rebukes and chasten. He said to be zealous, repent and turn to Him. If you feel His rebuke and feel that He is chastening you, it is because He loves you and wants you to sit with Him on His throne. This is His heart felt earnest desire for all of us. This comes down to an individual acceptance. Jesus Christ is standing at the door (outside the church) knocking. He will not impose Himself on anyone. If any man will hear His voice, and open the door (your heart and assembly), He will come in and sup with him. Unfortunately, some will not hear, because they are lukewarm.

The Laodicea church does not take a stand for righteousness. This is the age where the church is being tolerant and politically correct, and not biblically correct. They crave fame, acceptance and riches. Many have turned away from the Cross. They have forgotten the main reason Christ died on the Cross. Christ did not die so that human can obtain riches in this world. He died that we might have everlasting life. Some will gain riches in the world in honest ways. They will not let their riches deceive them into thinking that because they are rich they are righteous. It has become a tragedy in the church when monetary wealth is being preached as godliness, forgetting that Jesus tells us in St. Matthew 16:24, "Then said Jesus unto his disciples, if any man will come after me, let him deny himself, and take up his cross, and follow me." It was not money that was used as nails to nail Jesus Christ to the cross. It was not money that was used to make a crown that they placed on his head. It was a crown made of thorns that pierced His brow. Jesus Christ did not die that we may gain a worldly inheritance. We cannot be His disciples if we do not deny ourselves, take up our cross and follow Him. The cross represents suffering, pain, and death. Pick up your cross, preach and live the Word.

The Laodicea church equates righteousness with riches. They appeared to be anointed because they increased with goods. They seemed to be men and women of God because they have need of nothing and know how to speak well. They preach money, land, cars, houses, wealth, and mix in a bit of Jesus Christ in it, all in the name of Jesus Christ. They seek for themselves a place of notoriety, and have not given the true testimony of Jesus Christ to the unsaved. They are not faithful and true witnesses of Jesus Christ. They love to preach gain and harvest, while making merchandise of God's people. 2 Peter 2:3, "And through covetousness shall they with feigned words make merchandise of you: whose judgement now of a long time lingereth not, and their damnation slumbereth not." Jesus Christ in Revelation 3:14 said, "And unto the angel of the church of the

Laodiceans write; These things saith the Amen, the faithful and true witness, the beginning of the creation of God." "The Amen" stated that the Laodicea church was what He said it was. "The faithful and true witness, the beginning of the creation of God" is Jesus Christ. Laodicea church did not have the faithful and true witness in it, they had forgotten Him. He was outside knocking at the door. They had walked away from the faithful and true witness, the One who holds all things in His hands. The Laodicean angel, who is preaching and focusing on material increase, is not the true testimony of Jesus Christ.

This doctrine of devils and seducing spirits is designed to keep you from the power of the cross. 1 Timothy 4:1-2, "Now the Spirit speaketh expressly, that in the latter times some shall depart from the faith, giving heed to seducing spirits, and doctrines of devils; Speaking lies in hypocrisy: having their conscience seared with hot iron:" The goal of Satan is to keep them rich in material things and in poverty in Christ. Be not ignorant of the devil's devices. Many elevated Laodicean angels who preach cannot help a more needy assembly in ministering to them, because the price is not right. They need to have a specific type of accommodation that fits their lifestyle and a certain figure in dollars. The lesser assembly cannot pay for their required fees. They forgot

Jesus Christ paid the price on the cross for our salvation, to redeem man from sin. Jesus Christ, the beginning of the creation of the God, the one who made all things. St. John 1:3, "All things were made by him: and without him was not anything made that was made." They excluded the total works of redemption of Jesus Christ from their preaching. They omit repentance of sins, water baptism by total submersion in Jesus' name and the infilling of the Holy Ghost as it is written in the Word of God. They neglect to preach that there is a lake of fire reserved for all disobedience and a heaven to gain for all who accept the redemptive work on the cross. Revelation 20:7-8, "He that overcometh shall inherit all things; and I will be his God, and he shall be my son. But the fearful, and unbelieving, and the abominable, and murderers, and whoremongers, and sorcerer, and idolater, and all liars, shall have their part in the lake which burneth with fire and brimstone: which is the second death."

Many of these angels of the church have become motivational speakers inspiring us to become the best us. It is what we have become that is the problem. We are all to become like Jesus, pure and holy as He is. We are not to become selfish and devilish. Without holiness no man shall see God. We are called to be holy and called to be saints. Anytime the truth is mixed with a lie it becomes a lie. Man cannot redeem himself. Man cannot be redeemed with silver, gold or money. The atonement of Jesus Christ is excluded, and self-rectitude is being preached. We have become greedy, lovers of pleasure, and disciples of positive thinking. Having a form of godliness, professing to know God, but do not manifest Him. We have become powerless. Now, it is positive thinking and self-improvement instead of faith in God. Romans 1:17, "...The just shall live by his faith." It is not the just shall live by positive thinking. No longer allowing the blood of Jesus to blot out our sins, we have now turned to creative ways of self-improvement. We have turned to listen to the teachers of the world who profess worldly wisdom and have not given ourselves to faith in the Word of God. According to James 3:15, "This wisdom descendeth not from above, but is earthly, sensual, devilish."

Laodicean angels are leading people down the path of greed and destruction. Now we have a church of spiritual whores, full of envy, unsatisfied, unthankful, covetous, jealous and full of strife. They are piercing and selling their souls while trying to accumulate material things but reaping only sorrows, bitterness, ill feelings, and sleepless nights. They are becoming slaves to lenders and cannot connect to God, having their mind and spirit in torment. Many, who have not acquired the standard of prosperity, feel less fortunate and less blessed if they have not increased in goods. Some end up condemning themselves because they feel faithless. The apostle Paul warned Timothy in 2 Timothy 3:1-7 about these last days that we are living in. In his letter, Paul gave explicit details of the characteristics of this time period. The Bible declares in St. Matthew 7:16 that you shall know them by their fruit. In other words, their actions will reveal who they are.

Angels of the church should not be found guilty of encouraging their members to borrow money from credit cards, putting them in debt. In doing so, this will endorsed the borrower being a slave to the lender, putting them in bondage. Proverbs 22:7, "The rich ruleth over the poor, and the borrower is servant to the lender." People are not to be compelled to get what they cannot afford. This will only trap them in a world of debt, forcing them to service this debt. They end up doing everything in their power to pay it off, causing them to miss worship service. The debt has now become a god. Jesus is outside knocking to come in, the saints don't let Him in because they can't hear the knock. The saints are too busy serving their debts and mediating on their debts, wondering how they will make the payments. The saints now do not have any time to meditate on Jesus Christ.

The word and witness of Jesus Christ is committed to the angels of the church. The saints follow their teaching. Angels of the church will give account to God for everyone that was committed to his care. How have the angels of the church of Christ transmitted and transferred their spirits of greed and envy to the people? Whatever spirit you are of, that is the spirit you are transferring to the congregation. The angel of the Laodicea church was so far gone that Jesus brought it down to "if any man will hear His voice." It came down to an individual decision. It is not the will of God that any one should perish but that all should come to repentance and have everlasting life. Listen to the Lord Jesus Christ as He knocks, open the door to your heart and let Him in. Opening the door to let in the Lord Jesus Christ, means one will be totally committed to Him. All self will have to be denied and die daily, so that the individual's body truly becomes the temple of Christ. We have left our first love. Let us return to the love of Jesus Christ. Let us be zealous for Jesus Christ and repent. He is calling us back to Him.

17

Conclusion of the Matter

One day I came upon a spider's web. I felt strongly to move closer to it and to observe the web. I observed a bee trapped in the web. The bee was struggling, trying to be free but only got more and more entangled in the web. I looked at another side of the web and there was a small spider about five times smaller than the bee, quietly waiting. I wanted to do something to free the bee from the web. Someone came over to where I was and watched with me. I said to her I want to free the bee for I felt a saddened doom for this bee. The bee could in no way help himself to be free. He was doomed. She said to me that nature has to take its course. I knew then that I had to leave it alone. The spider sat there and watched as the bee struggled. I thought about how powerful this bee was, but was helpless in the web of the spider. About two days after, I went back and the bee was not moving anymore. In fact it did not look like a bee. I couldn't see the beautiful yellow and black stripes that it had so gloriously paraded. It was so pitiful that my heart went out towards it. I watched as the spider took its time and slowly ate away at the bee. This was the fate of the bee trapped in the web the spider had spun. I was emotionally disturbed by it and couldn't dismiss it from my thoughts.

After observing this course of nature, this thought came to me strongly. This is what Satan does to people. He gets them tangled up in his lies and sins, which engulfs and kills them like a fire that is set around a house with a person trapped inside. A little sin leads to more and more sin; resulting in total entanglement in sin to the point the person cannot find a way out of it. Satan mercilessly destroys them bit by bit, until they are unrecognizable. My heart was greatly saddened by this thought. I was allowed to feel the sad plight of the bee because the Lord wanted me to understand the predicament of those who are caught in Satan's web.

This has been a very doctrine-quaking word. God's thought for us is to come to the full knowledge of Jesus Christ. His agenda is abundant life. This word has come to set us free from the devil's web. It is not God's will for us to give the members of our body over to devils to carry out their plan to destroy us. Let us turn the members of our body over to Jesus Christ for He will abundantly pardon us.

Many assemblies have plummeted into gross darkness through comprise. Some are already deceived. They say that they are winning the world for Christ. They have put off Christ and have assimilated themselves with the world in order to win the world. Now they are identified with the world and not with Christ. They think they are winning the world for Christ, but in actuality it is the world that is winning them for the devil. The only Light is Jesus Christ. Let him back into the churches and follow His ways. Let the focus of our worship be to the Ever Living God and not to the pulpit. Offer to God the sacrifice of genuine worship in spirit and truth. Our bodies are His temple. Be a living temple for Him to dwell. Offer to God a temple that is suitable for His accommodation. Awake out of slumber. It is time to be sober and watchful. Be vigilant, relentless and diligent in our walk with the Lord. Be on guard at all times. We are of the day and not of the night. Don't let the day of the Lord come upon us unaware. Hold on to your crown.

Guard your heart with all diligence. Keep a watch over your spirit. We all have the power of choice, to choose what we allow into our heart. We have the power to reject what we don't want inside of us. We have it in us to choose. Reject the spirit of envy and all that comes with it. Embrace the spirit of "power, love and a sound mind." (2 Timothy 1:7) Let us indulge ourselves in the mind of Christ. Stay in line with the Word of God. Check your course. Remain connected to Jesus Christ. Eliminate all interference into your relationship with God. If you are one that is found in Satan's bed, get out with haste. Do not linger in his bed and question whether or not you should. Break all ties to Satan and his kingdom. Reject his fancies. Walk away from his flatteries. Refuse to be associated with him. Eradicate him from your life. Disallow his lies. Decline his offers. Throw out everything that he gave you and keep nothing. Don't put anything of the enemy to "rest in peace." They need to "rest in pieces," crushed and destroyed once and for all, with no possibility of resurrection. Turn to God with all of your heart. Remember your first love, Jesus Christ.

Return to God in water baptism, which is an essential part of salvation. Let our baptismal pools be active for the Kingdom. Bring in the souls. Allow them to be born again through the water and the Spirit, so that they can enter into the Kingdom of God. Receive the Holy Spirit with the evidence of speaking in tongues. This act of receiving the Spirit is crucial for the kingdom of God. Romans 8:9, "But ye are not in the flesh, but in the Spirit, if so be that the Spirit of God dwell in you, Now if any man have not the Spirit of Christ, he is none of his." We need to be full of the Holy Spirit. The Book of Acts stated repeatedly that the apostles were full of the Holy Spirit. They had an initial filling on the day of Pentecost with the evidence of speaking in other languages that they did not learn. Those who are being led by the Spirit of God are the sons of God according to Romans 8:14. We need to have the Spirit of God to be sons of God. How can one be led of the Holy Spirit when he does not have the Holy Spirit? One does not receive the Holy Spirit when he raises his right hand and says the "sinners' prayer," if there is no speaking in tongues as evidence. God's requirement remains the same in every generation.

Those who are in leadership must preach the true Word of God. Produce fruits of righteousness. If you are producing rotten fruits, go back to the Word of God. Teach the people to observe and do what is written in the Holy Bible. Check your soil. Check your heart. See exactly what you are producing. One can only produce what they sowed. Maybe what you are producing is not what is required then check what you are planting. Ensure that you are passing on to the saints that which is holy. God's judgement has already started on the nations. He has taken out the measuring stick and we are found short. Let us repent and return to Him. Wherever we have found ourselves lacking, let us take stock and come to the full measure of Christ. While His judgement is being outpoured, let us get ourselves in full alignment with His Word before it falls on us.

Keep a very close watch on our children. They are a heritage of the Lord, according to Psalms 127:3. They are God's precious gift to us. Let us show God our appreciation for His gifts and foster these children in God. Take time out to care for their well being, both temporal and spiritual. Don't leave them up to the electronics to foster and educate them. The children need to know that they are loved and cared for. One of the ways of showing them love is by not allowing them to do, as they want to do. It is not in them to direct their way. Take up your parental authority and right to ensure they fostered fully. This is our responsibility. Give them back to God by educating them in the things of God. They need to know that God created them for His glory. Prevent their involvement in the works of the devil. His aim is to utterly damage them from their early stages of life. It is hard to repair the damage done. Take the lead and let them follow you in righteousness.

Sow seeds of righteousness only. For whatever we plant, that is what we will reap. Put away witchcraft and the likes of it. Stop giving your hearts to evil. Don't allow Satan in, for he will stay in and won't leave. Study the Word of God, so that you will know how to live and speak the Word. Pray always for the saving of souls and not for the destruction of the soul. Fasting is good for the soul. We don't need to be caught up in evil practices. Let us come out from among these things and give ourselves over to righteousness. There is a spiritual law that works every time, the law of sowing and reaping. Those who do evil will reap evil. Those who sow good will reap the good they have sown. We don't need to revenge anyone who does evil to us. Their own evil desire for us will turn around and cause them to reap it. You will heap coals of fire on your enemy's head, when you do good things to him. Leave vengeance to God. Read about Haman's plot and doom in the Book of Esther. Sometimes you get slapped on one cheek. Turn the other cheek. In other words, turn around and do something good to the one that caused you hurt instead of returning evil to him or her.

Pay attention to the gospel of Jesus Christ. See to it that we do not water it down in order to accommodate our desire to be saved our way. Let's not be found guilty of adding and subtracting from the Word of God. We cannot change God's prescribed Word. Let us join forces with God and not with the devil. If you are serving money, repent and serve God. We are not to put anything in the place where God should be in your life.

May our hearts be opened to Jesus Christ. He is outside knocking to come in. Let Jesus in. He wants to come in and have sweet fellowship with us. I strongly encourage everyone and myself to let Jesus Christ into our lives and into the assemblies. "Let us hear the conclusion of the whole matter: Fear God, and keep his commandments: for this is the whole duty of man. For God shall bring every work into judgement, with every secret thing, whether it be good or whether it be evil" Ecclesiastes 12:13-14.

18

Repentance Call

Come, let us cry: "Search me, O God, and know my heart; and try me, and know my thoughts; and see if there be any wicked way in me, and lead me in the way everlasting" Psalms 139:23-24. The Lord Jesus Christ cares for His church. He is not willing for any of us to perish but that all repent and be saved. Let us increase our devotion and allegiance to Him. Focus on having the character of Jesus Christ and to be filled with all the fullness of God. Repentance and forgiveness are gifts of God for all humanity that we daily have access to. Use them up generously. The Lord pities His children. He waits for us to come to Him as a father looks out for his child. Let us bow our hearts before Him and allow Him to sit on the throne of our hearts. In worship, give Him of ourselves in spirit and in truth. Offer to Him the sacrifice of praise and thanksgiving. Give Him the fruit of our lips. Draw near to Him with a pure and sincere heart. Take up the Cross and follow him. Turn away from offering ourselves to the enemy. Turn back to our God. He will forgive us and abundantly pardon. 2 Chronicles 7:14, "If my people, which are called by my name, shall humble themselves, and pray and seek my face, and turn from their wicked ways; then will I hear from heaven and forgive their sin, and will heal their land."

Open the door of our hearts and let Jesus Christ back in the church. Then the glory of the Lord will be on us and our darkness will disappear. Put away the evil of our doings. Refuse to fellowship with unclean spirit. Put away the whoredom and the sorcery. Feast upon His Words. Lay aside every weight and besetting sin. God will help us to run the race with patience, (Hebrews 12:1). Come let us agree with David and take the cup of salvation and call on the name of the Lord, (Psalms 116:13). Reject the lies of the devil. We have been delivered from the powers of darkness and are translated into the Kingdom of Jesus Christ, (Colossians 1:13). Get back to preaching the Cross. Lift up Jesus, so that the world can see Him. He will draw all men to Him, (St. John 12:32). Seek Him first and His righteousness. He promised He would add all things to us (St. Matthew 6:33). Let us stop trying in our human efforts to add these things to ourselves without His help. He will supply all our needs according to His riches in glory, according to Philippians 4:19. He is able to do exceeding abundantly above all that we ask or think according to the power that works in us, as stated in Ephesians 3:20. Bring gifts worthy for repentance (St. Matthew 3:8). Psalms 95:6-8 says, "O come, let us worship and bow down; let us kneel before the Lord our maker. For he is our God; and we are the people of his pasture, and the sheep of his hand. Today if ye will hear his voice, Harden not you heart, as in the provocation, and as in the day of temptation in the wilderness:" If you hear His voice, don't harden your heart. Let our hearts be tender towards Him. Saints of the Most High God, let us operate in the wisdom that is from above towards everyone. James 3:17-18 states, "But the wisdom that is from above is first pure, then peaceable, gentle, and easy to be entreated, full of mercy and good fruits, without partiality, and without hypocrisy. And the fruit of righteousness is sown in peace of them that make peace." See also St. Matthew 4:4.

To everyone who reads this book, God's desire for us is that we would repent and turn from all our wicked ways. Turn to God and He will abundantly pardon. His Word declares in Deuteronomy 30:19, "I call heaven and earth as witness this day against you, that I have set before you life and death, blessing and cursing: therefore choose life, that both you and your descendants may live." Those who don't know the Lord Jesus Christ, today is the best day to come to Him and choose life. In whatever state we are, today is the best day to come to Him. He is calling to us. He is knocking. He is stretching out His hands. Come let us return to Him. It is time to respond to Jesus Christ. We can choose to yield to His message or we can choose to ignore the message and walk away; either way, we must respond. Who in this church age is willing to come and take a stand? Who will abide in His tabernacle? Who will dwell in His holy presence? Who among us is willing to separate themselves to God? Who is willing to preach the truth no matter the cost? Are you the one who is ready to make this commitment to God? Is your soul worth this price? Are you now willing and ready to lay it all down for the cause of Jesus Christ? This is the time of decision. Come to Jesus, the way to salvation. Let us repent and truly be converted every one of us.

God restore and bless every one of you in Jesus' name. Amen.

19

Prayer of Repentance

Our Righteous Heavenly Father, we come to You with humble hearts in the name of our Lord Jesus Christ. We stand firm on Your word that there is no other God beside You. You have called us to holiness because you are Holy. You have chosen us before the foundation of the world in Christ Jesus that we should be holy and walk before You blameless in love. Lord, Your word declares that You are not willing to have any of us perish but Your desire is that all should come to repentance and have eternal life. We come to You in humbleness of mind and spirit. We acknowledge our sins for they are great. Father, it is through the blood of Jesus that we have forgiveness of sins. Thank you for the blood of Jesus Christ that cleanses from all sins. Thank you for our advocate, Jesus Christ. We ask that the blood of Jesus Christ would wash and cleanse us from every one of these sins and even from those that were not addressed in this book. Cleanse us, Father from our individual sins and collective sins, as the body of Christ.

Father, we want to be holy as You are holy. Open the eyes of our understanding so that we may walk worthy of our calling and make our election sure. We desire to do Your will and follow You whole-heartedly, so we don't become a castaway. Father, give us the spirit of wisdom and revelation in the knowledge of Jesus Christ. We need to know and understand the hope of our calling. We need Your help in these areas, our God. Father, it is not in man to direct his ways. We turn to Your guidance so that Your light may shine on our path and give us clarity and truth.

Heavenly Father we agree with Hosea 14 and take up words of repentance. We return to the Lord our God. Forgive, O Lord, our unfaithfulness. We have dealt wickedly with our neighbours, please forgive us. We have deceived our brothers and sisters, please forgive us. Our iniquities have caused us to fall. Our love has gone cold because of the increase of our iniquities. Father, a broken and contrite heart You will not despise. We cry to You Father, to forgive all our iniquities and receive us graciously, so we may offer You the praise of our lips. The world cannot save us neither can our riches save us.

We refuse to listen any longer to seducing spirits and doctrines of devils. We will no longer give ourselves to be a participant in the works of the devil. We are sorry for our sins. We cut all ties with the devil. Our bodies we present as a living sacrifice to You, let it be holy and acceptable to You, our Father. Father, we thank You for forgiveness. Now let Your will be done in us as it is done in heaven. Thank You for receiving us, in Jesus name.

1 Timothy 1:17, "Now unto the king eternal, immortal, invisible, the only wise God, be honour and glory for ever and ever. Amen."

About the Author

Sonia R. Anderson was born in Jamaica W. I. and grew up in Toronto, Canada. Upon entry to Canada the gospel of Jesus Christ was preached to her and she received Jesus Christ as her Lord and Savior at the age of thirteen. Sonia is the mother of three children and grandmother of two. She is a Registered Early Childhood Educator and Writer. Sonia has served in various ministering positions and administrative capacities in the church over several years Her mission in life is to minister the Word of Truth to people everywhere.

www.ingramcontent.com/pod-product-compliance
Lightning Source LLC
Chambersburg PA
CBHW051755040426
42446CB00007B/383